Development and Design of Heritage Sensitive Sites

This book provides a framework for assessing the development potential of heritage sensitive sites within the context of national policy. Until now, architectural books on conservation matters have tended to focus on preservation at a strategic level and restoration at a technical level. This book offers the architect, developer or planner the rules and tools needed to gauge development prospects in an objective and comprehensive manner.

Written by an experienced expert in the field it provides the reader with:

- the latest legislation relating to Listed Buildings and Conservation Areas and other built heritage issues in the UK
- an insight into local planning authorities' and government advisory boards' involvement
- basic strategies for approaching the development of heritage sensitive sites
- an understanding of the options available
- a basic framework for the presentation of heritage cases
- illustrative case studies highlighting strategic success.

This book provides a one-stop shop for any professional or student working in, or learning about, development in heritage sensitive environments.

Kenneth Williamson is a partner in the Hurd Rolland Partnership, an architectural practice located in London, Manchester and Scotland. He is in charge of a specialist consultancy section dealing with listed buildings and built heritage issues and has provided strategic heritage advice in relation to a number of urban regeneration projects throughout Scotland. He has wide-ranging design and contractual experience encompassing projects for local authority, central government and private sector clients.

Development and Design of Heritage Sensitive Sites

Strategies for Listed Buildings and Conservation Areas

Kenneth Williamson

Routledge
Taylor & Francis Group

LONDON AND NEW YORK

First published 2010
by Routledge
2 Park Square, Milton Park, Abingdon, Oxon, OX14 4RN

Simultaneously published in the USA and Canada
by Routledge
270 Madison Avenue, New York, NY 10016

Routledge is an imprint of the Taylor & Francis Group, an informa business

© 2010 Kenneth Williamson

Typeset in Galliard and Univers by
Florence Production Ltd, Stoodleigh, Devon
Printed and bound in Great Britain by
TJ International Ltd, Padstow, Cornwall

British Library Cataloguing in Publication Data
A catalogue record for this book is available from the British Library

Library of Congress Cataloging-in-Publication Data
Williamson, Kenneth.
   Development and design of heritage sensitive sites: strategies for listed
   buildings and conservation areas/Kenneth Williamson.
      p. cm.
   Includes index.
   1. Historic buildings – Conservation and restoration – Great Britain.
   2. Historic sites – Conservation and restoration – Great Britain.
   3. Cultural property – Protection – Great Britain – Planning.
   4. Great Britain – Cultural policy.   I. Title.   II. Title: Strategies
   for listed buildings and conservation areas.
   NA109.G7W56 2010
   363.6′90941 – dc22   2009053639

ISBN13: 978–0-415–48643–9 (hbk)
ISBN13: 978–0-415–48644–6 (pbk)
ISBN13: 978–0-203–84843–2 (ebk)

For my father, Ian Williamson

Contents

Contents

Illustration credits

Cover photographs of Quartermile, courtesy of David Williamson.

Glasgow City Archives and Special Collections, The Mitchell Library, Culture and Sport Glasgow: Figures 3.6, 3.8, 3.13 and 3.16.

Reproduced by permission of the Trustees of the National Library of Scotland: Figures 1.9a and b, 1.10a and b, 1.11, 1.12, 1.14, 1.15, 3.4, 3.5 and 3.10–3.12.

Reproduced by permission of Ordnance Survey on behalf of HMSO © Crown copyright 2010. All rights reserved. Ordnance Survey Licence number 100049743: Figures 1.19, 2.3–2.5, 2.14 and 3.2.

The author would like to thank the following organizations for their kind assistance:

    Allan Murray Architects
    Archial Architects
    East Dunbartonshire Council
    Havelock Europa
    House of Fraser
    Hurd Rolland Architects
    Mountgrange
    Muse Developments.

Foreword

Manish Chande

Urban environments, as particularly evidenced by cities and towns, have evolved their built form over time in response to those inhabiting them, whether for work, rest or play. Like living organisms, these environments continue to evolve as each new generation tries to reshape them to meet its own needs and agendas, while the built environment of yesterday becomes our heritage. It is, therefore, hardly surprising that the interface between development of the new and the conservation of the old needs careful navigating, otherwise it quickly becomes an area of friction.

Therefore development within a heritage-sensitive environment needs to be shaped, not only by a clear understanding of how that environment has evolved over very many years, but also by a clear understanding of the legal and planning policy framework that underpins how any such development will be assessed.

Although major planning decisions are political and, almost always, ultimately subjective, the underlying assessment must be objective and show a balance between the need to conserve and the need to allow development that benefits the health and vibrancy of the city or town concerned. For the developer to lead the planning process toward his own optimum development solution, he must be able to justify his proposals in terms of the established legal and planning policy framework, as well as articulate his vision.

The methodological approach to assessing heritage issues described in this book was that taken in our successful planning application for Caltongate, which involved proposals for the regeneration of a highly sensitive site in the heart of Edinburgh's Old Town.

Preface

There are very few instances where major regeneration proposals for an existing urban centre will not affect Listed Buildings and/or Conservation Areas. This book is intended to provide a structured approach to the not inconsiderable design and planning issues that require to be addressed.

As it reflects my own direct experience in relation to a number of major projects undertaken in central Edinburgh and Glasgow, and elsewhere in Scotland, the legal framework and national policy and guidance applying in Scotland provide the principal points of reference. However, the controlling principles discussed essentially reflect the relevant statutory provisions and national policy and guidance existing throughout the UK. In this respect, I have endeavoured to set these out in terms of both the Scottish and English policy frameworks.

Part 1

Controlling principles

Introduction

The relevant statutory provisions and national policy and guidance relating to development affecting the historic built environment are generally directed toward preservation. However, importantly, they are set within a context that acknowledges the necessity of beneficial change. In this regard, they provide the essential framework for developing appropriate design and planning strategies.

Creative control of any proposed development and its evolution through the planning process is based on informed decision-making, which must be controlled by the developer if the compromises that inevitably arise are to be minimized. In this regard, where Listed Buildings and Conservation Areas are concerned, it is essential for developers and those promoting regeneration to understand the controlling principles, and how they will affect the scope of any development, prior to entering into discussions with either the local planning authorities or the relevant statutory bodies.

As a rule of thumb, where Listed Buildings and Conservation Areas (and other statutorily protected heritage assets, such as Scheduled Monuments) form part of an application site, these are primary issues that require to be given high priority within the design process from the outset.

Within Part 1, I have outlined the key controlling principles that are relevant to the consideration of development proposals affecting the historic built environment.

Chapter 1

Planning hierarchy

The hierarchy of controlling principles for development affecting Listed Buildings and Conservation Areas in the UK is:

- Acts of Parliament
- national planning guidance
- local planning policy.

In this respect, all strategies in relation to such development should ultimately be routed back to the requirements of the Acts.

Acts of Parliament

For the purposes of this book, the principal relevant Acts are as follows:

England and Wales

- Town and Country Planning Act 1990.
- The Planning (Listed Buildings and Conservation Areas) Act 1990.

The long-awaited Heritage Protection Bill, which was intended comprehensively to overhaul existing legislation in England and Wales, was put on hold for the time being at the end of 2008.

Scotland

- Town and Country Planning (Scotland) Act 1997.
- Planning etc. (Scotland) Act 2006.
- The Planning (Listed Buildings and Conservation Areas) (Scotland) Act 1997.

These Acts provide the statutory framework governing all planning decisions relating to Listed Buildings and Conservation Areas throughout mainland UK.

In each case, the Acts refer to the 'Secretary of State' as the principal authority. In current parlance, in England this refers to the Secretary of State for Culture, Media and Sport, and, in Wales and Scotland, the National Assembly for Wales and the Scottish Government, respectively. The administration of 'Secretary of State' function in each case is undertaken by English Heritage (the Historic Buildings and Monuments Commission for England), in England; the Historic Building Advisory Council for Wales, in Wales; and Historic Scotland, in Scotland.

In Northern Ireland, the essential legal principles are similar to elsewhere in the UK; however, the administration of the planning process varies significantly. The relevant statutory instrument is the Planning (Northern Ireland) Order 1991.

National planning guidance

In both England and Scotland the key national planning guidance has recently been updated. In Scotland, National Planning Policy Guidance (NPPG) 18 was initially superseded by Scottish Planning Policy (SPP) 23 in October 2008. SPP 23 was subsequently superseded by the all encompassing Scottish Planning Policy (SPP) in February 2010. The first version of the Scottish Historic Environment Policy (SHEP) properly came into being in October 2008 but, along with the still evolving Managing Change in the Historic Environment suite of documents, only fully superseded the long established Memorandum of Guidance on Listed Buildings and Conservation Areas in July 2009.

In England, PPG 15 – which had been the principal source of national guidance for over 15 years – was superseded by Planning Policy Statement (PPS) 5, in March 2010. In both instances the new guidance seeks to encompass all historic built environment designations.

The key national planning guidance referred to here is as follows:

England

- Planning Policy Statement 5: Planning for the Historic Environment (PPS 5).
- Planning Policy Statement 5: Planning for the Historic Environment – Historic Environment Planning Practice Guide (PPS 5 Practice Guide).

National policy guidance for Wales is provided by Welsh Office Circulars 61/96 and 1/98.

Scotland

- Scottish Planning Policy (SPP) – February 2010.
- Scottish Historic Environment Policy (SHEP) – July 2010.
- Managing Change in the Historic Environment.

It should be noted that while the form and breadth of content within the new guidance has changed quite dramatically from that of its predecessors, it is still underpinned by the long standing Planning (Listed Building and Conservation Areas) Acts on either side of the border.

Local planning policy

Regional and local authorities are legally bound to produce (and regularly update) regional and local development plans that set out local planning policy in detail. Requirements in this regard are set out in a wide variety of Planning Acts and specific national guidance. However, within this essential framework, specific local policy is established by individual authorities after extensive public consultation.

Regarding Listed Buildings and Conservation Areas, regional and local authorities are bound to make provision for the requirements of the above legislation and guidelines within their own structure and local plans. Consequently, it is generally the case that local planning policy affecting Listed Buildings and Conservations Areas largely follows national policy.

However, national policy directs that local authorities make certain detailed provisions, particularly in relation to Conservation Areas. In this regard, specific detailed guidance produced at local level may include:

- planning briefs and other forms of supplementary planning guidance;
- Conservation Area appraisals.

Beyond specific conservation policy, published local policy can identify the wider aspirations and formal policies associated with specific sites and local areas, against which cases for beneficial development might be set. This is of particular significance for a developer seeking to justify development within a heritage-sensitive environment.

The local and structure plans for most areas throughout the UK are generally available through the relevant local authority website.

Chapter 2

Listed Buildings

Within the Planning (Listed Buildings and Conservation Areas) Acts, Listed Buildings are defined at Section 1:

> For the purposes of this Act and with a view to the guidance of local planning authorities in the performance of their functions under this Act and the principal Act in relation to buildings of special architectural or historic interest, the Secretary of State shall compile lists of such buildings . . .

Listing is essentially a state designation. In practice, principally English Heritage (the Historic Buildings and Monuments Commission for England), the Historic Building Advisory Council for Wales and Historic Scotland select the buildings and structures of special architectural or historic interest that are to be included on the lists, generally following the systematic survey and resurvey of particular areas, or on the recommendation of local planning authorities.

In England and Wales, listed buildings and structures are categorized by English Heritage as follows:

- Grade I
- Grade II*
- Grade II

as an indication of their relative importance.

In Scotland, Historic Scotland uses the following categories:

- A: buildings of national or international importance, either architectural or historic, or fine, little altered examples of some particular period style or building type;
- B: buildings of regional or more than local importance, or major examples of some particular period, style or building type;

- C(S): buildings of local importance; lesser examples of any period, style or building type, as originally constructed or altered; and simple, traditional buildings that group well with others.

In neither case does the category of listing carry any statutory weight. In this regard, the legislation set out in the Acts applies to all listed buildings equally. In England, this presently extends to around 500,000 buildings (only 6 per cent of which are Grade I or II*).

There are a wide range of duties in relation to Listed Buildings set out within the Planning (Listed Buildings and Conservation Areas) Acts. For the purposes of development strategy, the single most important is the general duty on a planning authority in exercising planning functions, as follows:

England and Wales

66 General duty as respects listed buildings in exercise of planning functions
(1) In considering whether to grant planning permission for development which affects a listed building or its setting, the local planning authority or, as the case may be, the Secretary of State shall have special regard to the desirability of preserving the building or its setting or any features of special architectural or historic interest which it possesses . . .

Scotland

59 General duty as respects listed buildings in exercise of planning functions
(1) In considering whether to grant planning permission for development which affects a listed building or its setting, a planning authority or the Secretary of State, as the case may be, shall have special regard to the desirability of preserving the building or its setting or any features of special architectural or historic interest which it possesses . . .
(3) In this section, 'preserving', in relation to a building, means preserving it either in its existing state or subject only to such alterations or extensions as can be carried out without serious detriment to its character, and 'development' includes redevelopment . . .

Essentially, this directs that, in determining a planning application affecting Listed Buildings, the desirability to preserve what is of special architectural or historic interest is to be given a high level of importance over other related planning issues under consideration by the relevant planning authority. This may be the special interest of the building in its entirety, the setting of the building or identifiable features of the building.

In this respect, it can be seen that a proper understanding of what is of special architectural or historic interest is essential to creating a competent development strategy. The listing descriptions provided by English Heritage and the information supplementary to the statutory list provided by Historic Scotland, although not to be considered definitive, are a useful starting point.

Chapter 3

Conservation Areas

Regarding Conservation Areas, the Planning (Listed Buildings and Conservation Areas) Acts direct, under Section 69 in England and Section 61 in Scotland, that:

> Every local planning authority –
>
> (a) shall from time to time determine which parts of their area are areas of special architectural or historic interest the character or appearance of which it is desirable to preserve or enhance; and
>
> (b) shall designate those areas as conservation areas.

Conservation Areas are essentially local authority designations, although, in certain circumstances, a Conservation Area can be designated by central government.

For our purposes, two general duties on local authorities are significant:

England and Wales

71 Formulation and publication of proposals for preservation and enhancement of conservation areas

(1) It shall be the duty of a local planning authority from time to time to formulate and publish proposals for the preservation and enhancement of any parts of their area which are conservation areas.

(2) Proposals under this section shall be submitted for consideration to a public meeting in the area to which they relate.

(3) The local planning authority shall have regard to any views concerning the proposals expressed by persons attending the meeting.

72 General duties as respects conservation areas in exercise of planning functions

(1) In the exercise, with respect to any buildings or other land in a conservation area . . . special attention shall be paid to the desirability of preserving or enhancing the character or appearance of that area.

Scotland

63 Proposals for preservation and enhancement of conservation areas

(1) It shall be the duty of a planning authority to formulate and publish, from time to time, proposals for the preservation and enhancement of any parts of their district which are conservation areas.

(2) Proposals under this section shall be submitted for consideration to a public meeting in the area to which they relate.

(3) The planning authority shall have regard to any views concerning the proposals expressed by persons attending the meeting.

64 General duty as respects conservation areas in exercise of planning functions

(1) In the exercise, with respect to any buildings or other land in a conservation area . . . special attention shall be paid to the desirability of preserving or enhancing the character or appearance of that area.

As with Listed Buildings, the general duty in the exercise of planning functions establishes that, in considering planning applications affecting a Conservation Area, the desirability of preserving or enhancing the character or appearance of the area is to be given a higher level of importance.

The duty on a local authority to produce proposals for the preservation and enhancement of conservation areas, generally in the form of Conservation Area Appraisals and Supplementary Planning Guidance, provides a locally adopted benchmark against which any development proposals require to be assessed.

Chapter 4

Other relevant designations

There are a number of other statutory and non-statutory designations affecting the built environment. Whereas, previously, guidance in relation to such designations had been relatively disparate, in England, PPS 5 now essentially provides a single over-arching policy approach that encompasses all such designations as Heritage Assets. In Scotland, while the updated guidance in SPP and SHEP now provides a similar umbrella, the evolution from previous guidance has been much less dramatic.

Examples of other statutory and non-statutory designations include:

Statutory

- Scheduled Monuments
- designated wreck sites.

Non-statutory

- World Heritage Sites (WHS)
- historic parks and gardens (in England); gardens and designed landscapes (in Scotland).

Statutory

Scheduled Monuments

Scheduled Monuments are protected under the Ancient Monuments and Archaeo-logical Areas Act 1979. In practical terms, scheduling is undertaken by the same national bodies responsible for listing buildings on behalf of the relevant Secretary of State. The critical controlling legislation states:

2 Control of works affecting scheduled monuments

(1) If any person executes or causes or permits to be executed any works to which this section applies he shall be guilty of an offence unless the works are authorised under this Part of this Act.

(2) This section applies to any of the following works, that is to say –

   (a) any works resulting in the demolition or destruction of or any damage to a scheduled monument;

   (b) any works for the purpose of removing or repairing a scheduled monument or any part of it or of making any alterations or additions thereto; and

   (c) any flooding or tipping operations on land in, on or under which there is a scheduled monument.

(3) Without prejudice to any other authority to execute works conferred under this Part of this Act, works to which this section applies are authorised under this Part of this Act if –

   (a) the Secretary of State has granted written consent (referred to below in this Act as 'scheduled monument consent') for the execution of the works; and

   (b) the works are executed in accordance with the terms of the consent and of any conditions attached to the consent.

Essentially, any proposed work that physically affects a Scheduled Monument requires Scheduled Monument Consent. Applications for such consent are made direct to the relevant Secretary of State.

In England, planning guidance previously provided in PPG 16: Archaeology and Planning, has now been subsumed into the holistic guidance now provided by PPS 5: Planning for the Historic Environment. Similarly, in Scotland the relevant planning guidance is now provided in SPP and SHEP. In both cases, beyond the statutory requirements under the Ancient Monuments and Archaeological Areas Act 1979, the guidance provides that the protection of a scheduled monument and its setting is a material consideration in any planning application under the Town and Country Planning Acts.

Designated wreck sites

This is clearly a very specific designation and will only have relevance to potential development within UK coastal waters.

Designation is made under the Protection of Wrecks Act 1973. Section 1(2) of the Act states:

An order under this section shall identify the site where the vessel lies or formerly lay, or is supposed to lie or have lain, and –

(a) the restricted area shall be all within such distance of the site (so identified) as is specified in the order, but excluding any area above high water mark of ordinary spring tides; and

(b) the distance specified for the purposes of paragraph (a) above shall be whatever the Secretary of State thinks appropriate to ensure protection for the wreck.

The type of protection required is envisaged in Section 1(3):

a person commits an offence if, in a restricted area, he does any of the following things otherwise than under the authority of a licence granted by the Secretary of State –

(a) he tampers with, damages or removes any part of a vessel lying wrecked on or in the sea bed, or any object formerly contained in such a vessel; or

(b) he carries out diving or salvage operations directed to the exploration of any wreck or to removing objects from it or from the sea bed, or uses equipment constructed or adapted for any purpose of diving or salvage operations; or

(c) he deposits, so as to fall and lie abandoned on the sea bed, anything which, if it were to fall on the site of a wreck (whether it so falls or not), would wholly or partly obliterate the site or obstruct access to it, or damage any part of the wreck;

(d) and also commits an offence if he causes or permits any of those things to be done by others in a restricted area, otherwise than under the authority of such a licence.

Non-statutory

World Heritage Sites

The Convention Concerning the Protection of the World Cultural and Natural Heritage was adopted by UNESCO in 1972. Since that time, the World Heritage Committee has inscribed almost 900 sites on a World Heritage List.

Article 4 of the Convention states:

Each State Party to this Convention recognizes that the duty of ensuring the identification, protection, conservation, presentation and transmission to future generations of the cultural and natural heritage referred to in Articles 1 and 2 and situated on its territory, belongs primarily to that State. It will do all it can to this end, to the utmost of its own resources and, where appropriate, with any international assistance and co-operation, in particular, financial, artistic, scientific and technical, which it may be able to obtain.

The UK adopted the Convention in 1984. As a signatory, the duty in relation to the built environment is primarily embodied in the already existing legislative and national policy framework described above. In this regard, WHS status carries no additional statutory protection. However, current national planning guidance in the UK acknowledges WHS status as a material planning consideration.

PPS 5: Planning for the Historic Environment

> 3. The policies in this PPS are a material consideration which must be taken into account in development management decisions, where relevant . . .

> HE9.1 There should be a presumption in favour of the conservation of designated heritage assets . . . Substantial harm to or loss of designated heritage assets of the highest significance, including . . . World Heritage Sites, should be wholly exceptional.

The practice guide to PPS 5 states:

> 98. World Heritage Sites are nominated by the Government for inscription onto the UNESCO World Heritage List on account of their Outstanding Universal Value (OUV), authenticity and integrity. CLG Circular 07/09: Protection of World Heritage Sites and accompanying English Heritage guidance sets out the roles and responsibilities of local planning authorities in protecting, promoting, interpreting, sustainably using and conserving World Heritage Sites and their OUV and settings. Circular 07/09 requires local planning authorities to place due weight upon the need to protect all aspects of the OUV when planning decisions are made.

SPP: Scottish Planning Policy

> 120. World Heritage Sites are inscribed by UNESCO as cultural and/or natural heritage sites which are of outstanding universal value. Planning authorities should protect World Heritage Sites and their settings from inappropriate development, including relevant policies in the development plan and setting out the factors that will be taken into account when deciding applications for development proposals which may impact on a world heritage site.

> 121. World heritage site management plans should be prepared which summarise the significance of the site and set policies for the protection and enhancement of the site. Planning authorities should consider incorporating the management plan into the development plan as supplementary guidance.

There are now over twenty-five sites in the United Kingdom. A current list and access to information on each site can be found at www.culture.gov.uk/ukwhportal/index.htm.

Major planning applications affecting a World Heritage Site can become controversial and hard fought. In extreme cases local and national decision making can be brought under the scrutiny of UNESCO.

Historic parks and gardens/gardens and designed landscapes

Guidance regarding the protection of designed landscapes is included within both PPS 5 and SPP.

PPS 5: Planning for the Historic Environment

> HE9.1 There should be a presumption in favour of the conservation of designated heritage assets ... Substantial harm to or loss of designated heritage assets of the highest significance, including grade I and II* registered parks and gardens ... should be wholly exceptional.

The practice guide to PPS 5 notes:

> Registered parks and gardens are designated by English Heritage under the Historic Buildings and Ancient Monuments Act 1953 for their special historic interest.

SPP: Scottish Planning Policy

> 122. An Inventory of Gardens and Designed Landscapes of national importance is compiled by Historic Scotland. Relevant policies should be included in local development plans. The effect of a proposed development on a garden or designed landscape should be a consideration in decisions on planning applications.

Such designations are particularly significant when considering new development in town and city centres throughout the UK, where, during the late nineteenth century, there was a philanthropic trend toward providing public parks.

> Other non-statutory designations include battlefields, for which registers and inventories are maintained by both English Heritage and Historic Scotland, and at a less well defined level the wider historic landscape and other historic environment interests.
> It is a critical element of site analysis to establish all heritage designations that affect a site from the outset. Developments affecting statutory designations have to be addressed in accordance with the relevant legislation. Developments affecting non-statutory designations generally require to be addressed as material planning considerations by Local Authorities and can become extremely controversial.

Chapter 5

Listed Buildings and Conservation Areas under the planning process

The planning process is defined in the Acts of Parliament and national planning guidance referred to above. An outline of the key procedures relating to Listed Buildings and Conservation Areas is given here.

It is of fundamental importance to recognize that practical control of the planning process is undertaken at local level by local authority planning departments. Applications for planning consent are submitted to the relevant planning authority, whose officers consider it in terms of the pertinent specific local planning policy (which, as discussed above, is led by national planning policy). Planning applications generally require to be advertised and to be notified to owners and tenants of adjacent properties. Consequently, public consultation is an inherent part of the process.

Under the Section 8 of the Planning (Listed Buildings and Conservation Areas) Act in England and Wales, and Section 7 in Scotland, Listed Building consent is required for:

- the alteration or extension of a listed building;
- the demolition of a listed building.

Under Sections 74 and 66 of the respective Acts, Conservation Area consent is only required for the proposed demolition of an unlisted building or structure within a Conservation Area.

It is very rarely the case that Listed Building or Conservation Area consent will be given without a detailed understanding of the proposed new development in the form of a detailed planning application. Indeed, it is unusual for consent for demolition to be granted without a reciprocal detailed consent for what is to replace it. Generally, applications for Listed Building and/or Conservation consent are dealt with in parallel with an associated planning application. All local authorities should publish relevant pro forma in this respect.

Planning departments, under certain circumstances, are required to consult with various statutory bodies as part of the planning process. In relation to planning applications for development affecting Listed Buildings and Conservation Areas, in England and Wales, under Section 15(5) of the Act and Section 15 of Circular 01/01, local planning authorities are required to consult with English Heritage under the following circumstances:

outside Greater London:

- for works in respect of any Grade I or II* listed building;
- for works for the demolition of a principal Grade II (unstarred) listed building; or
- for works for the alteration of any Grade II (unstarred) listed building that comprise or include:
    - the demolition of a principal external wall of the principal building;
    - the demolition of all or a substantial part of the interior of the principal building.

in Greater London:

- for works in respect of any Grade I or II* listed building;
- for works for the demolition of a principal Grade II (unstarred) listed building;
- for works in respect of any principal Grade II (unstarred) listed building that is a railway station (including an underground railway station), theatre, cinema or bridge across the Thames;
- for works in respect of any curtilage building to a principal Grade II (unstarred) building that is a railway station (including an underground railway station);
- for works in respect of any Grade II (unstarred) listed building that is owned by a local planning authority in its area and where the application is made by a person other than the authority;
- for works for the alteration of any Grade II (unstarred) listed building that comprise or include:
    - the demolition of a principal external wall of the principal building;
    - the demolition of all or a substantial part of the interior of the principal building.

Under Circular 09/05, notice of applications for Listed Building consent and of the decisions taken by local planning authorities requires to be given to:

- the Ancient Monuments Society
- the Council for British Archaeology
- the Georgian Group
- the Society for the Protection of Ancient Buildings

- the Victorian Society
- Twentieth Century Society

in relation to planning applications for:

(a) the demolition of a listed building; or
(b) the alteration of a listed building that comprises or includes the demolition of any part of that building.

Under Sections 67 and 60 of the respective Acts on either side of the border, where an application includes proposals that would, in the opinion of the authority, affect the setting of a listed building, local planning authorities are required to publish a notice to this effect. Thereafter, they are required to take into account any representations essentially in accordance with normal planning procedures.

It should be noted that, in Scotland, under Section 13(3) of the Planning (Listed Buildings and Conservation Areas) Act, Historic Scotland are to be consulted on planning applications where these affect the site and setting of Category A Listed Buildings, Scheduled Monuments and gardens and designed landscapes included in the inventory.

Beyond these statutory consultees, individual planning authorities may choose to consult with any number of local conservation groups.

After full consideration of an application by the relevant planning department, a recommendation for acceptance or refusal will be made to the local authority planning committee, comprising elected local councillors. Generally, decisions are taken at full meetings of the planning committee, which are open to the public, although, in some predetermined situations, decisions will be taken under delegated powers.

In England and Wales, Section 13 of the Planning (Listed Buildings and Conservation Areas) Act states:

13 Duty to notify Secretary of State of applications

(1) If a local planning authority (other than a London borough council) to whom application is made for listed building consent, or a London borough council to whom such an application is made by the Commission, intend to grant listed building consent they shall first notify the Secretary of State of the application, giving particulars of the works for which the consent is required.

In Scotland, this is stated under Section 12 of the Act:

12 Duty to notify Secretary of State of applications

(1) If a planning authority to whom application is made for listed building consent intend to grant such consent they shall first notify the Secretary of State of the application giving particulars of the works for which the consent is required.

In both cases, this essentially means that a local planning authority cannot finally grant Listed Building consent without the sanction of the Secretary of

State/Scottish government. The requirements vary for development proposed in Greater London, but the sanction of the Secretary of State is still ultimately required (Circular 01/01 identifies various situations where applications, generally relating to proposals affecting Grade II (unstarred) buildings, do not required to be notified).

The process of notification is administered by English Heritage, the Historic Building Advisory Council and Historic Scotland. The Acts indicate that the Secretary of State has a period of 28 days to direct the application to him for decision, to notify the local authority that he does not intend to do this, or to advise that he will require further time.

It is relatively unusual for the Secretary of State to require that an application for Listed Building consent be referred to him for decision, but where proposals raise issues of exceptional significance or are highly controversial an application may be called in. In such circumstances, the related planning application will also be called in. Where an application is called in, a public local inquiry is almost always held prior to the Secretary of State making the final decision.

Local authorities are empowered to grant final consent if:

- the Secretary of State has notified them that he does not intend to require the reference of the application; or
- notification of an extension to the 28 day period is not given.

Where a local authority is proposing to undertake works that require Listed Building or Conservation Area consent, such applications are, in any event, to be decided by the relevant Secretary of State.

Chapter 6

Listed Building issues

The key issues affecting Listed Buildings in relation to development are:

- demolition
- alteration
- setting.

Demolition

National planning guidance is clear regarding the presumption that no listed building should be demolished. However, this is qualified by tests against which justification for demolition can be set.

PPS 5

In England, previous guidance specifically relating to the demolition of listed buildings has been replaced by all encompassing guidance covering development affecting heritage assets in general. The new specific guidance in PPS 5 covering the potential demolition of a listed building, or any heritage asset, is included in policy HE9:

> HE9.1 There should be a presumption in favour of the conservation of designated heritage assets and the more significant the designated heritage asset, the greater the presumption in favour of its conservation should be. Once lost, heritage assets cannot be replaced and their loss has a cultural, environmental, economic and social impact. Significance can be harmed or lost through alteration or destruction of the heritage asset or development within its setting. Loss affecting any designated heritage asset should require clear and convincing justification. Substantial harm to or loss of a grade II listed building, park or garden should be exceptional. Substantial harm to or loss of designated heritage assets of the highest significance, including scheduled monuments, protected wreck sites, battlefields, grade I and II* listed buildings and grade I and II* registered parks and gardens, World Heritage Sites, should be wholly exceptional.

HE9.2 Where the application will lead to substantial harm to or total loss of significance local planning authorities should refuse consent unless it can be demonstrated that:

(i) the substantial harm to or loss of significance is necessary in order to deliver substantial public benefits that outweigh that harm or loss; or

(ii) (a) the nature of the heritage asset prevents all reasonable uses of the site; and

(b) no viable use of the heritage asset itself can be found in the medium term that will enable its conservation; and

(c) conservation through grant-funding or some form of charitable or public ownership is not possible; and

(d) the harm to or loss of the heritage asset is outweighed by the benefits of bringing the site back into use.

PPS 5 continues:

HE9.3 To be confident that no appropriate and viable use of the heritage asset can be found under policy HE9.2(ii) local planning authorities should require the applicant to provide evidence that other potential owners or users of the site have been sought through appropriate marketing and that reasonable endeavours have been made to seek grant funding for the heritage asset's conservation and to find charitable or public authorities willing to take on the heritage asset.

HE9.4 Where a proposal has a harmful impact on the significance of a designated heritage asset which is less than substantial harm, in all cases local planning authorities should:

(i) weigh the public benefit of the proposal (for example, that it helps to secure the optimum viable use of the heritage asset in the interests of its long-term conservation) against the harm; and

(ii) recognise that the greater the harm to the significance of the heritage asset the greater the justification will be needed for any loss.

SHEP

In Scotland, in contrast to the more wordy approach previously utilised in the now superseded Memorandum of Guidance, the updated policy set out in SHEP states:

3.40 Once lost listed buildings cannot be replaced. They can be robbed of their special interest either by inappropriate alteration or by demolition. There is, therefore, a presumption against demolition or other works that adversely affect the special interest of a listed building or its setting.

3.42 Knowing what is important about a building is central to an understanding of how to protect its special interest. Applications should demonstrate that in arriving at a strategy for intervention, the importance of the building has been clearly understood and those features which contribute to its special interest have been identified . . .

3.50 In the case of applications for the demolition of listed buildings it is Scottish Ministers' policy that no listed building should be demolished unless it can be clearly demonstrated that every effort has been made to retain it. Planning authorities should therefore only approve such applications where they are satisfied that:

a.   the building is not of special interest; or

b.   the building is incapable of repair; or

c.   the demolition of the building is essential to delivering significant benefits to economic growth or the wider community; or

d.   the repair of the building is not economically viable and that it has been marketed at a price reflecting its location and condition to potential restoring purchasers for a reasonable period.

Additional, more detailed guidance is contained in *Managing Change in the Historic Environment: Demolition*. It should be noted that the recently published guidance on both sides of the border now tacitly accepts that the demolition of a Listed Building may be justified on the basis that it is essential to delivering substantial public benefits that outweigh its loss.

While the updated guidance on both sides of the border has modified previous guidance, justification for the demolition of a Listed Building is still essentially made under the following broad headings:

* importance
* condition
* alternative use
* benefits of redevelopment.

Alterations

Alterations to Listed Buildings are to be considered in terms of the building's sustainable continued use. National guidance is provided to limit alterations to those absolutely necessary and to prevent or reduce the impact of such changes on the special interest of the building.

PPS 5

In PPS 5 alterations to Heritage Assets are also dealt with in policy HE9.

3.12 Many listed buildings are already in well-established uses, and any changes need be considered only in this context. But where new uses are proposed, it is important to balance the effect of any changes on the special interest of the listed building against the viability of any proposed use and of alternative, and possibly less damaging, uses. In judging the effect of any alteration or extension it is essential to have assessed the elements that make up the special interest of the building in question . . .

3.13 Many listed buildings can sustain some degree of sensitive alteration or extension to accommodate continuing or new uses . . . Nevertheless, listed buildings do vary greatly in the extent to which they can accommodate change without loss of special interest . . .

3.15 Achieving a proper balance between the special interest of a listed building and proposals for alterations or extensions is demanding and should always be based on specialist expertise; but it is rarely impossible, if reasonable flexibility and imagination are shown by all parties involved. Thus, a better solution may be possible if a local planning authority is pre-pared to apply normal development control policies flexibly; or if an applicant is willing to exploit unorthodox spaces rather than set a standard-ized requirement; or if an architect can respect the structural limitations of a building and abandon conventional design solutions in favour of a more imaginative approach . . . The preservation of façades alone, and the gutting and reconstruction of interiors, is not normally an acceptable approach to the re-use of listed buildings: it can destroy much of a building's special interest and create problems for the long-term stability of the structure.

SHEP

Again, the guidance in SHEP has been stripped back, stating:

3.49 Where a proposal involves alteration or adaptation which will have an adverse or significantly adverse impact on the special interest of the building, planning authorities, in reaching decisions should consider carefully:

a. the relative importance of the special interest of the building; and
b. the scale of the impact of the proposals on that special interest; and
c. whether there are other options which would ensure a continuing bene-ficial use for the building with less impact on its special interest; and
d. whether there are significant benefits for economic growth or the wider community which justify a departure from the presumption set out in paragraph 3.42 above.

Setting

Where a proposed development site contains a Listed Building or has Listed Buildings located nearby, the impact of the proposed development on the setting of the Listed

Building(s) is often the more pressing consideration. This is particularly the case when higher-category listings (Grade I or II* or Category A or B) are involved.

PPS 5

Regarding development affecting the setting of a Heritage Asset, PPS 5 states:

> HE10.1 When considering applications for development that affect the setting of a heritage asset, local planning authorities should treat favourably applications that preserve those elements of the setting that make a positive contribution to or better reveal the significance of the asset. When considering applications that do not do this, local planning authorities should weigh any such harm against the wider benefits of the application. The greater the negative impact on the significance of the heritage asset, the greater the benefits that will be needed to justify approval.

> HE10.2 Local planning authorities should identify opportunities for changes in the setting to enhance or better reveal the significance of a heritage asset. Taking such opportunities should be seen as a public benefit and part of the process of placeshaping.

In Scotland, setting is referred to in very general terms in SHEP.

SHEP

Regarding the setting of Category A and B Listed Buildings, SHEP states:

> 3.55 When considering a developer's proposals to integrate listed buildings into an overall development, Ministers expect planning authorities to take into account not only the desirability of preserving the building's historic fabric but the need to maintain it in an appropriate setting. Planning authorities involved in discussions about work to Category A and B listed buildings, that is novel, contentious or large scale, should consult with Historic Scotland at an early stage.

Annex 7 to SHEP states:

> 6. Under section 59(1) of the 1997 Act the planning authority, in determining any application for planning permission for development that affects a listed building or its setting, is required to have special regard to the desirability of preserving the building, or its setting, or any features of special architectural or historic interest which it possesses.

> 7. Planning authorities must consult Scottish Ministers in respect of applications under the Town and Country Planning (Scotland) Act 1997 that affect a Category A listed building or its setting (Town and Country Planning (General Development Procedure) (Scotland) Order 1992).

Additional, more detailed guidance is contained in *Managing Change in the Historic Environment: Setting*. All of the above issues require to be taken into account when the assessment of impact on Listed Buildings in relation to a development project is being undertaken. This is considered further at Part 2: Assessment.

Chapter 7

Conservation Area issues

The key issues relating to Conservation Areas are:

- the preservation or enhancement of the Conservation Area;
- demolition of unlisted buildings within a Conservation Area.

In this respect the latter is effectively dealt with in terms of preservation or enhancement.

Preservation or enhancement

Assessing preservation or enhancement is tied into establishing the essential character and appearance of the Conservation Area.

PPS 5

The new guidance in PPS 5 again largely incorporates the key guidance regarding Conservation Areas under the generic guidance at HE9 regarding Heritage Assets. Some specific guidance is provided at HE9.5, which states:

HE9.5 Not all elements of a World Heritage Site or Conservation Area will necessarily contribute to its significance. The policies in HE9.1 to HE9.4 and HE10 apply to those elements that do contribute to the significance. When considering proposals, local planning authorities should take into account the relative significance of the element affected and its contribution to the significance of the World Heritage Site or Conservation Area as a whole. Where an element does not positively contribute to its significance, local planning authorities should take into account the desirability of enhancing or better revealing the significance of the World Heritage Site or Conservation Area, including, where appropriate, through development of that element. This should be seen as part of the process of place-shaping.

It is interesting to note the equivalence given in the updated guidance to Conservation Areas and World Heritage Sites.

SPP

In Scotland SPP notes:

> 115. Conservation areas are areas of special architectural or historic interest, the character or appearance of which it is desirable to preserve or enhance. Their designation provides the basis for the positive management of an area. A proposed development that would have a neutral effect on the character or appearance of a conservation area (i.e. does no harm) should be treated as one which preserves that character or appearance. The design, materials, scale and siting of new development within a conservation area, and development outwith the conservation area that will impact on its appearance, character or setting, should be appropriate to the character and setting of the conservation area. Planning permission should normally be refused for development, including demolition, within a conservation area that fails to preserve or enhance the character or appearance of the area.

It should be noted that, although there is a requirement within the Planning (Listed Buildings and Conservation Areas) Acts for local authorities to formulate and publish from time to time proposals for the preservation and enhancement of Conservation Areas within their area of control, and some guidance within both PPS 5 and SPP regarding defining the character and appearance of Conservation Areas, it is often the case that there is little formal basis upon which to assess the impact of a development proposal on the character and appearance of a Conservation Area. In such situations, credible independent assessment is required.

PPS 5

PPS 5 avoids actual reference to Conservation Area Appraisals as such. Relevant generic guidance is included at HE2 and HE3.

Current English Heritage guidance on Conservation Area management and appraisals is set out in *Guidance on the Management of Conservation Areas* and *Guidance on Conservation Areas Appraisals*, both published by English Heritage in 2005.

SPP

In Scotland, SPP states:

> 117. Planning authorities are encouraged to undertake conservation area appraisals. PAN 71 Conservation Area Management provides good practice

for managing change, sets out a checklist for appraising conservation areas and provides advice on funding and implementation.

The Annex to Planning Advice Note (PAN) 71 Conservation Area Management sets out a formalized approach to Conservation Area appraisals.

Demolition of unlisted buildings

Under the Planning (Listed Buildings and Conservation Areas) Acts, Conservation Area consent is required for the demolition of unlisted buildings within a Conservation Area.

PPS 5

In PPS 5 the effect that the demolition of unlisted buildings will have on a Conservation Area is covered by the cross-reference in policy HE9.5 to HE9.1–HE9.4 and HE10.

SPP

In Scotland, SPP states:

> 116. Conservation area consent is required for the demolition of unlisted buildings in conservation areas. The merits of the building and its contribution to the character and appearance of the conservation area are key considerations when assessing demolition proposals. Where demolition is considered acceptable, careful consideration should be given to the design and quality of the replacement scheme. More information on conservation area consent is provided in SHEP.

SHEP, in fact, provides little further detail in this respect.

Again, defining the character and appearance of the Conservation Area is of critical importance.

Chapter 8

Benefits of development

In terms of the Planning (Listed Buildings and Conservation Areas) Act, the general duty in the exercising of planning function is that special regard/attention is to be paid to the *desirability* of preserving, and so on. That is to say, preservation is the desired intent. The Act, however, does not obviate consideration of the benefits that can be derived from development.

Notwithstanding the extensive statutory provisions and guidance on the protection of the historic built environment, there is general acknowledgement, borne out within the relevant guidance, that new development can significantly benefit the long-term future of such environments.

PPS 5

In this regard, PPS 5 states:

> HE7.5 Local planning authorities should take into account the desirability of new development making a positive contribution to the character and local distinctiveness of the historic environment . . .

> HE9.4 Where a proposal has a harmful impact on the significance of a designated heritage asset which is less than substantial harm, in all cases local planning authorities should:

> (i) weigh the public benefit of the proposal (for example, that it helps to secure the optimum viable use of the heritage asset in the interests of its long-term conservation) against the harm; and

> (ii) recognise that the greater the harm to the significance of the heritage asset the greater the justification will be needed for any loss.

SPP

SPP notes:

> 111. In most cases, the historic environment (excluding archaeology) can accommodate change which is informed and sensitively managed, and can be adapted to accommodate new uses whilst retaining its special character. The aim should be to find a new economic use that is viable over the long term with minimum impact on the special architectural and historic interest of the building or area.

Of much greater significance, it must be noted that the relevant guidance goes beyond this. As indicated in the section above relating to Listed Building issues, under both PPS 5 and SHEP, the demolition of a Listed Building can now, in principle, be justified solely on the basis that its loss is essential to delivering substantial public benefits.

Stepping back from this more extreme position, it can be seen that the current relevant planning guidance requires decision makers to weigh the desirability of wholesale preservation of the existing historic built environment against the social, economic and cultural benefits of any proposed development.

Part 2

Assessment

Introduction

The assessment of impact on the historic built environment must be firmly rooted in the essential statutory provisions protecting that environment. That is, in relation to Listed Buildings:

> In considering whether to grant planning permission for development which affects a listed building or its setting, the local planning authority or, as the case may be, the Secretary of State shall have special regard to the desirability of preserving the building or its setting or any features of special architectural or historic interest which it possesses.

And, in relation to Conservation Areas:

> In the exercise, with respect to any buildings or other land in a conservation area ... special attention shall be paid to the desirability of preserving or enhancing the character or appearance of that area.

The impact of development in these terms is ultimately the central basis for all planning decisions regarding Listed Buildings and Conservation Areas and is considered in detail in a raft of documents published by English Heritage and Historic Scotland, including:

- *Conservation Principles: Policies and Guidance for the Sustainable Management of the Historic Environment*, published by English Heritage in April 2008.
- *Conservation Plans: A Guide to the Preparation of Conservation Plans*, published by Historic Scotland in 2000
- *Seeing the History in the View: A Method for Assessing Heritage Significance within Views*, draft published by English Heritage in April 2008.
- *Guidance on the Management of Conservation Areas*, published by English Heritage in August 2005.

- *Guidance on Conservation Area Appraisals*, published by English Heritage in August 2005.
- PAN 71 *Conservation Area Management Annex: Conservation Area Appraisal*, published by the Scottish Executive in December 2004.

However, from the developer and decision-maker's standpoint, as set out in Chapter 8, impact has to be considered within the context of the social, economic and cultural benefits that are to be derived from any proposed development. A basis for assessing the benefits of development is not adequately provided for within current standardized assessment methodologies, which generally tend toward the assessment of impact and preservation in isolation. In presenting a full case for Listed Building and/or Conservation Area consent, it can be seen that a bespoke approach to assessment that specifically considers both identifiable impacts and derived benefits is required.

Within this part of the book, I have outlined a series of issues that require be considered in relation to developing an integrated approach to assessment for the purposes of making a case for Listed Building and/or Conservation Area consent, under the following broad chapter headings:

Significance

Chapter 9: Historical background
Chapter 10: Identification of heritage assets
Chapter 11: Special interest of a Listed Building
Chapter 12: Setting of a Listed Building
Chapter 13: Character and appearance of a Conservation Area

Impact

Chapter 14: Impact of development on heritage assets
Chapter 15: Environmental impact assessment

Benefits

Chapter 16: Benefits of development

Chapter 9

Historical background

The start point of any assessment of any site located within a historic built environment is to establish its historical context. The simplest and most graphic means of doing this is to use published historic plans and OS maps as a framework and to overlay these with any specific further research undertaken. This will provide a visual progression of how any area has developed over many years.

In the United Kingdom the first edition of the national OS maps was published from around the 1850s and updated regularly thereafter on around a twenty-year cycle. In many instances, these alone will provide a sufficient historical matrix.

Local libraries can yield historic maps and plans that were prepared much earlier than this. For major developments within long-established urban settings, such information, properly analysed, can provide an informed visual record of how a place has developed over hundreds of years.

Thereafter, depending on the nature of the assessment, other useful information can be gleaned from:

- local authority building warrant and planning archives – drawings, and so on;
- local and regional libraries – historical photographs, local histories, and so on;
- newspaper archives.

Whereas, in England and Wales, information tends to be decentralized, in Scotland, the National Map Library provides a useful single source of historic maps and plans for all of Scotland. Similarly, the Royal Commission on the Ancient and Historical Monuments of Scotland (RCAHMS) holds a useful national archive of drawings and photographs.

It is important to remain focused on the physical development of the area being assessed, although clearly this will also reflect relevant social and economic history. Research is time consuming and can lead to very many interesting historical distractions that can ultimately hold less real value in terms of the assessment of the built environment.

The assessment of historical background should always culminate in an assessment of the present physical context of the site. A photographic survey of key elements, combined with up-to-date OS information, will again provide a strong visual record.

It can be readily understood that a very delapidated area will potentially benefit substantially from regeneration. Similarly, an environment that has been subjected to years of utilitarian development can be improved by a higher quality of design.

The historical, physical context of a site can provide a relevant basis for design decisions regarding the setting of buildings and also regarding the natural evolutionary path of the wider area into which the design proposal is to be integrated.

Chapter 10

Identification of heritage assets

Once a site boundary and a broad development proposal are established, a trawl of all heritage assets that are likely to be affected requires to be undertaken. This includes, not only assets that will be physically or directly impacted upon, but, equally, immediately adjacent and more distant assets whose settings will potentially be affected.

In a city- or town-centre location, it is often the indirect impact on the setting of adjacent Listed Buildings or the character and appearance of Conservation Areas that will potentially be most significant. Similarly, development outwith but adjacent to a Conservation Area may potentially impact upon its character and appearance.

It should be noted that, as the form of any proposed development evolves, and the potential impacts become more defined, there will be a requirement to reconsider the list of heritage assets that may be affected.

I have included below a broad list of statutory and non-statutory heritage assets that may come under consideration.

Statutory

- Scheduled Monuments
- Listed Buildings
- Conservation Areas
- protected wreck sites.

Non-statutory

- World Heritage Sites
- historic parks and gardens (in England)/gardens and designed landscapes (in Scotland)

- historic battlefields
- historic landscapes.

For the purposes of this book, I have specifically focused on Listed Buildings and Conservation Areas. In practice, the impact on all heritage assets will require to be assessed using a similar methodology.

Useful Internet access to comprehensive information locating and describing Listed Buildings includes:

In England

Heritage Gateway (www.heritagegateway.org.uk/Gateway) provides links to:

> Listed Buildings Online (http://lbonline.english-heritage.org.uk)
> PastScape (http://pastscape.english-heritage.org.uk)
> Images of England (www.imagesofengland.org.uk).

In Scotland

Pastmap (www.rcahms.gov.uk/pastmap.html).

In line with the essentially local designation of Conservation Areas, there are no national databases in this regard. However, under their duty to publish proposals for the preservation and enhancement of Conservation Areas, most local authorities include detailed information on their websites under planning or conservation.

Once the Listed Buildings or Conservation Areas (or other designations) that will potentially be impacted upon have been identified, more detailed consideration of what constitutes the special interest or setting or character and appearance of these designations is required.

It should be understood that, although conservation issues are significant parameters that should inform the design of a development and be given special regard, there are many other parameters that have to be considered in reaching a viable development solution. If development is to take place at all, varying degrees of impact on the existing built fabric is inevitable. Again, it is a combination of the degree of impact and the extent to which development will bring social, economic and cultural benefits to the local or wider area that is the key determining factor.

Chapter 11

Special interest of a Listed Building

The statutory provision is clear that it is the preservation of the building or its setting, or any features of *special* architectural or historic interest that it possesses, that is to be given special regard. Indeed, in Scotland, this is specifically emphasized in SHEP, where it is stated:

> 2.32 Many buildings are of interest, architecturally or historically, but for the purposes of listing this interest must be 'special'. Listing is therefore assessed against a set of clear criteria which are set out in Annex 2.

PPS 5

Regarding assessment of significance PPS 5 states:

> HE6.1 Local planning authorities should require an applicant to provide a description of the significance of the heritage assets affected and the contribution of their setting to that significance. The level of detail should be proportionate to the importance of the heritage asset and no more than is sufficient to understand the potential impact of the proposal on the significance of the heritage asset. As a minimum the relevant historic environment record should have been consulted and the heritage assets themselves should have been assessed using appropriate expertise where necessary given the application's impact . . .

Practical advice regarding assessment is given with the practice guide to PPS 5:

> 55. Understanding the nature of the significance is important as it is vital to understanding the best means of conservation. A modern building of high architectural interest will have quite different sensitivities from an archaeological site where the interest arises from the possibility of human remains being buried there.

58. In accordance with HE6.1, an applicant will need to undertake an assessment of significance to an extent necessary to understand the potential impact (positive or negative) of the proposal and to a level of thoroughness proportionate to the relative importance of the asset whose fabric or setting is affected. Given the obvious burden of the process, local planning authorities will need to be careful to only ask the applicant for what is genuinely needed to satisfy the policy requirement. Although there is no limit on the sources of information that might be consulted or the exercises that might be carried out to fulfil that requirement, the most common steps an applicant might take are as follows. The first three steps will be undertaken in almost every case.

1. Check the development plan, main local and national records including the relevant Historic Environment Record, statutory and local lists, the Heritage Gateway, the NMR, and other relevant sources of information that would provide an understanding of the history of the place and the value the asset holds for society.

2. Examine the asset and its setting.

3. Consider whether the nature of the affected significance requires an expert assessment to gain the necessary level of understanding.

4. Consider whether there are any special techniques that need to be employed because of the type of asset.

5. Seek advice on the best means of assessing the nature and extent of any archaeological interest e.g. geophysical survey, physical appraisal of visible structures and/or trial trenching for buried remains.

6. Consider, in the case of certain buildings whether physical intervention, such as the removal of plaster, may be needed to reveal important details hidden behind later additions and alterations.

7. Carry out additional assessment where the initial research has established an architectural, historic, artistic and/or archaeological interest but the extent, nature or importance of which needs to be established more clearly before safe decisions can be made about change to the site. This may require a desk-based assessment and/or on-site evaluation. Such may be necessary for all types of asset, including buildings, areas and wreck sites, where understanding of the asset's history and significance is incomplete. Where applicants are to commission assessment or evaluation they are advised to discuss the scope of the work with the local planning authority in advance and to agree a written scheme of investigation, if necessary, before commencement.

8. Consider, and if necessary confirm, whether any investigative work may itself require planning permission or other consent.

The previous guidance set out in now superseded PPG 15 included a detailed description of the criteria and principles for selection of a Listed Building. This has not been carried over into the present guidance.

SHEP

In Scotland, the essential principles previously included in the now superseded Memorandum of Guidance, are largely incorporated in Annex 2 of SHEP:

3. The principles of selection for statutory listing are broadly:

a.   age and rarity;

b.   architectural or historic interest;

c.   close historical associations.

Age and rarity

4. The older a building is and the fewer of its type that survive the more likely it is to present a special interest. Age is a major factor in the evaluation process but its weight differs across the building types. Period definitions are given to facilitate the assessment but these are not intended to be watersheds or cut-off points.

5. All buildings erected before 1840 (pre-Victorian and the arrival of the railways) which are of notable quality and survive predominantly in their original form have a strong case. The year 1840 was selected because of the change which followed, in terms of the greater standardisation of materials and design, improved communications and the birth of the architectural press.

6. Buildings put up between 1840 and 1945 which are of special architectural or historic interest and of definite character either individually or as part of a group may be listed. As the survival rate increases after 1914, greater selectivity will be applied to take account of lesser rarity and relative age.

7. Those erected after 1945 may merit inclusion on the lists if their special architectural or historic interest is of definite architectural quality.

8. The listing of buildings less than 30 years old requires exceptional rigour because those making the judgement do not have the advantage of a long historical perspective. Threats to building types are often a trigger for advance consideration of buildings from this period.

Architectural or historic interest

9. Selection for architectural or historic interest is assessed under a range of broad headings, summarised below.

10. Interior: Interior design and fixed decorative schemes of houses or business premises in all their variation can add to the case for listing. Examples include skirting boards, plasterwork, dado rails, chimney-pieces, staircases, doors and over-door panels, ornate radiators, floor grilles, sanitary ware, the existence of box-beds, vaulted basement or wine cellar divisions, slate shelving, servant bell systems, shop or pub fittings and fixed internal machinery.

11. Plan form: The internal planning of buildings is instructive and can be ingenious although it may not be evident on the exterior. For example, the original flatting arrangement in terraced houses and tenements may not be obvious from the street and the plan of a farm steading, hospital or prison may reflect the latest theories in the design of each of these structures and therefore give the property additional significance.

12. Technological excellence or innovation, material or design quality: Evidence of structural or material innovation adds weight to a decision. Exceptional structural form can be significant and is found across the wide variety of building types from a cruck-framed barn to an early iron-framed jute mill or steel-framed office block. Exceptional use of materials or use of fine material may be a factor. Style will be considered against relevant conventions particularly for its quality or exceptional interest.

13. Setting: The context in which a structure sits can be a critical factor in its evaluation. It invariably accounts for its form and should not be under-rated. A structure whose setting has changed adversely, removing the original contextual character, or which has been removed from its context, has one less factor in support of its case for designation.

14. Regional Variations: The best examples of local vernacular buildings will normally be listed because together they illustrate the importance of distinctive local and regional traditions. It is important to ascertain distinctive regional variations in type, material and form.

Close historical association

15. Close associations with nationally important people, or events whose associations are well-documented, where the physical fabric of the building is also of some quality and interest, can be a significant factor. In consideration of such cases the association must be well authenticated and significant. The fabric should reflect the person or event and not merely be a witness to them. Local traditions are not always trustworthy. In most cases the building in question will have other qualities which combine to give it special interest, such as Walter Scott's house in Castle Street, Edinburgh, which forms part of a fine classical terrace. Where architectural interest is weak the case for listing on historical association must be strong. The building must be well preserved in a form and condition which directly illustrates its historical associations with the person or event in question. The transient association of short term guests, lodgers and tenants, however eminent, will not usually justify listing.

Working with the principles

16. In choosing buildings within the above broad principles:

a.   particular attention is paid to the special value within building types, either for architectural or planning reasons, or as illustrating social and economic history;

b.　a building may be listed for its contribution to an architecturally or historically interesting group, such as a planned burgh, town square or model village as well as its intrinsic merit considered in isolation;

c.　the impact of vernacular buildings in particular is often made not only by individual buildings but by their grouping. At the other end of the spectrum, a major country house may well be enhanced by adjacent buildings such as stables, lodges, gatepiers and bridges in its curtilage, and vice versa;

d.　authenticity, that is a building's closeness to the original fabric and therefore its ability to convey its significance, and levels of integrity, carries weight. It need not be the case that a building is as originally built, because changes made to it may have added to its significance. What is added or taken away will be considered for the overall benefit or detriment to its character.

17. It is important to stress that when buildings are being considered for listing, no factors other than architectural or historic interest as defined above can be taken into account. The condition of a property, for example, is not a factor in the evaluation unless it detracts significantly from the architectural or historic interest so that it can no longer be defined as special.

Listing information

English Heritage and Historic Scotland provide descriptions of buildings and structures that accompany the list as part of the listing process. It is important to note that this listing information is not to be considered a definitive account of the building's interest in a legal sense. It should, however, provide a sense of what has been considered important to its designation and is useable in this respect.

PPS 5

In PPS 5 there is no specific reference to list descriptions; rather there is a general reference to Historic Environment Records (HERs) as the relevant source of key information. In this respect the HER incorporates the list descriptions for Listed Buildings.

Information supplementary to the statutory list

In Scotland, listing information is published as information supplementary to the statutory list. In this regard, the information is prefaced by the statement: 'Information Supplementary to the Statutory List (this information has no legal significance).'

In the absence of specific legally binding definitions of why any individual Listed Building or structure has been designated, in order to assess the impact that any proposal will have on the special architectural or historic significance of a Listed Building, the developer is left with the task of either seeking independent specialist advice or relying on any expertise provided by the relevant local authority (most of whom have a designated conservation officer). In adopting the former approach prior to meeting with the local authority, the developer will generally have an advantageous, wider knowledge base going into any initial discussions.

In general, any contact with English Heritage or Historic Scotland will be initiated through initial discussions with the relevant local authority.

It should be considered that, although English Heritage and Historic Scotland are responsible for designating Listed Buildings, independent specialist assessment based upon the above criteria can yield a more detailed and up-to-date understanding of the architectural or historic significance of a specific building or group of buildings. Although consultation during the assessment process is essential to establishing the specific views held by these statutory bodies, the results should be considered in terms of the wider development parameters and concluded upon accordingly.

Given that the potentially most significant cultural benefit of new development is cross-funding the sustainable future use of Listed Buildings that are otherwise at risk, it is useful, in a situation where the listing includes a wide variety of structures over a wide curtilage, to grade the various elements in order of significance. This will assist in prioritizing the extent of conservation work that can be sustained and the amount of new development that is justifiable, and in promoting a reasonable balance between the two.

Chapter 12

Setting of a Listed Building

In environments populated by Listed Buildings, it is more often than not the impact upon the setting of listed buildings that becomes the critical issue.

In relation to Policy HE10, the practice guide to PPS 5 states:

> 113. Setting is the surroundings in which an asset is experienced. All heritage assets have a setting, irrespective of the form in which they survive and whether they are designated or not. Elements of a setting may make a positive or negative contribution to the significance of an asset, may affect the ability to appreciate that significance, or may be neutral.

Regarding the assessment of impact on setting the practice guide notes:

> 118. Change, including development, can sustain, enhance or better reveal the significance of an asset as well as detract from it or leave it unaltered. For the purposes of spatial planning, any development or change capable of affecting the significance of a heritage asset or people's experience of it can be considered as falling within its setting. Where the significance and appreciation of an asset have been compromised by inappropriate changes within its setting in the past it may be possible to enhance the setting by reversing those changes.

> 122. A proper assessment of the impact on setting will take into account, and be proportionate to, the significance of the asset and the degree to which proposed changes enhance or detract from that significance and the ability to appreciate it.

> 123. English Heritage is preparing detailed guidance on understanding the setting of heritage assets and assessing the impact of any changes affecting them and on how to assess heritage significance within views.

Managing Change in the Historic Environment: Setting

In recognition of its criticality in relation to planning matters, in Scotland, the previously less than well defined guidance regarding setting is now addressed in the Managing Change in the Historic Environment suite of documents. The relevant document regarding setting states:

> This note sets out the overarching principles that apply to developments affecting the setting of historic structures or places including scheduled monuments, listed buildings, parks/gardens/designed landscapes, World Heritage Sites, conservation areas, and designated wrecks. For the purpose of this note the term 'historic structure' is intended to cover all types of built heritage protected by these designations . . .

> **What is 'setting'?**

> Monuments, buildings, gardens and settlements were not constructed in isolation. They were deliberately positioned with reference to the surrounding topography, resources, landscape and other monuments or buildings. These relationships will often have changed through the life of a historic structure. Setting can be thought of as the way in which a historic structure's surroundings contribute to how it is experienced, understood and appreciated. Setting often extends beyond the immediate property boundary of a historic structure into the broader landscape.

> **What contributes to setting?**

> The setting of a historic structure can incorporate a range of factors, not all of which will apply to every case. These include:

> *   current landscape or townscape context;
> *   visual envelope, incorporating views to, from and across the historic structure;
> *   key vistas, framed by rows of trees, buildings or natural features that give a structure a context, whether or not intentional;
> *   the historic structure's prominence in views throughout the surrounding area;
> *   character of the surrounding landscape;
> *   general and specific views including foregrounds and backdrops;
> *   relationships between both built and natural features;
> *   aesthetic qualities;
> *   other non-visual factors such as historical, artistic, literary, linguistic, or scenic associations, intellectual relationships (e.g. to a theory, plan or design), or sensory factors;
> *   a 'Sense of Place': the overall effect formed by the above factors.

> Defining the setting of a historic structure will ultimately rely on profes-sional judgement based on a range of considerations, including those set

out in this section. The assessment of cultural significance must be rooted in a wider understanding of the historic environment. Both the definition of setting and the assessment of the impact of new development will be case specific.

The guidance continues by setting out a staged approach to assessing the impact of new development.

As with the Listed Buildings and their special architectural and historic interest, the assessment of the setting of Listed Buildings and the impact of development is ultimately one of specialist opinion and judgement framed in terms of the above guidance.

The interrelationship between a building and its surroundings may have changed dramatically over very many years. In this respect, it is not uncommon for a Listed Building to be surrounded by buildings of utilitarian quality, from later periods in an area's development, or, indeed, to stand within an area of long-term dereliction.

It should be acknowledged that the existing setting of the building might be very poor when considered alongside its original historic context. Nevertheless, it is the impact that any proposed development will have on the existing setting that requires to be assessed. Consequently, it can be seen that it may not be desirable to preserve the existing setting of a Listed Building if a more relevant setting can be reinstated or provided. Clearly, the desirability of change would have to relate to the considerations outlined above.

Where a number of equivalent Listed Buildings are located immediately adjacent to each other, a Georgian terrace might be a good example, the setting of the individual building becomes interrelated with the wider group. As a consequence, it is no longer the case that the individual building should necessarily remain the focus of its setting; rather, it is the impact that a proposed development would have on the existing whole.

Chapter 13

Character and appearance of a Conservation Area

In paying special attention to the desirability of preserving or enhancing the character or appearance of a conservation area, it is necessary, in the first instance, to establish what the character or appearance of the area is. It is good practice for local authorities to provide formal Conservation Area Appraisals for areas designated within their local plan area. However, it is very common to find that no such formal appraisal has been produced.

PPS 5

PPS 5 makes no specific reference to the provision of Conservation Area Appraisals. Again the general reference at HE6 to Historic Environment Records (HERs) as the relevant source of key information should be taken to encompasses any appraisal or other information that may exist.

SHEP

In Scotland, beyond the general guidance provided at paragraph 117 of SPP, SHEP states:

> 2.47. Scottish Ministers expect local authorities to designate only those areas which they consider to be of special architectural or historic interest as conservation areas. As part of this process they encourage them to undertake a thorough appraisal of any area before designation, to ensure that its character and appearance are properly understood. The criteria to be taken account of in designation are set out in Annex 3.

Annex 3, 'Criteria for the designation of Conservation Areas', states:

> 1. It is the character or historic interest of an area created by individual buildings and open spaces and their relationship one with the other which the legislation covering conservation areas seeks to preserve.

2. The statutory definition is 'areas of special architectural or historic interest the character or appearance of which it is desirable to preserve or enhance' and conservation areas will inevitably be of many different kinds. 3. The principles of selection for designation as a conservation area are broadly as follows:

a. areas of significant architectural or historic interest in terms of specific listed buildings and/or ancient monuments;
b. areas of significant architectural or historic interest in terms of building groupings, which may or may not include listed buildings and/or ancient monuments, and open spaces which they abut;
c. areas with features of architectural or historic interest such as street pattern, planned towns and villages and historic gardens and designed landscapes;
d. other areas of distinctive architectural or historic character.

4. In designating a conservation area, thought should also be given to the reasons why it is felt that it should be protected. These may include:

a. its special architectural and historic importance;
b. its distinct character;
c. its value as a good example of local or regional style;
d. its value within the wider context of the village or town;
e. its present condition and the scope for significant improvement and enhancement.

Beyond this, specific guidance on the preparation of Conservation Area Appraisals is provided in the following documents:

- *Guidance on Conservation Area Appraisals*, published by English Heritage in August 2005.
- PAN 71, *Conservation Area Management Annex: Conservation Area Appraisal*, published by the Scottish Executive in December 2004.

In practice, where the character and appearance of a Conservation Area, and what would be considered to preserve or enhance it, are not defined within a specific Conservation Area Appraisal, and this is very often the case, it is useful for an independent specialist assessment to be undertaken. The independent assessment may or may not use the methodology included in the above documents, but should clearly define:

- the character and appearance of the Conservation Area, and
- policy guidance set out in the relevant local and structure plan, including permissible land uses and any adopted supplementary planning guidance.

Where a Conservation Area Appraisal has been provided, this should be taken as formal definition in this regard. Key elements can be identified accordingly and can provide a definitive basis for the consideration of whether a proposal will be detrimental or will preserve or enhance the Conservation Area.

Chapter 14

Impact of development on heritage assets

In principle, the assessment of whether or not a development proposal will have an impact on a heritage asset is relatively straightforward. In the first instance, the special interest of the asset must be established, essentially as discussed above. Where alteration or demolition is being considered, the impact will be direct or physical. Where the setting of an asset will be altered, the impact will be indirect.

It can be seen that, taken in isolation, a development proposal will either impact upon the special interest of a heritage asset, or not. Thereafter, consideration of whether any impact is beneficial or detrimental or will have a neutral effect is required.

Beneficial impacts

Beneficial impacts include, for example:

- the restoration of elements of a Listed Building;
- the improved setting of a Listed Building;
- the enhancement of a Conservation Area.

Detrimental impacts

Examples of detrimental impacts include:

- the demolition of a Listed Building;
- detracting from the setting of a Listed Building;
- the demolition of an unlisted but significant building within a Conservation Area.

Neutral impacts

Neutral impacts might include:

- the demolition or alteration of a Listed Building that would have no effect on features of special architectural or historic interest;
- a development within a Conservation Area that results in the preservation of the existing character or appearance of that area.

In smaller-scale developments, a bespoke approach to the consideration of impact as part of an overall Heritage Statement provides a useful precursor to the consideration of the benefits of development. Certain types of development are considered to be Environmental Impact Assessment (EIA) development. Such development requires impact to be assessed under the more empiric format laid down in the relevant regulations.

Chapter 15

Environmental impact assessment

Where an EIA is required under the Town and Country Planning (Environmental Impact Assessment) (England and Wales) Regulations 1999 and the Environmental Impact Assessment (Scotland) Regulations 1999, then the impact of a proposal on heritage assets is generally considered in the cultural heritage chapter of the EIA submitted with the application for planning consent.

Town and Country Planning (Environmental Impact Assessment) (England and Wales) Regulations 1999

In England and Wales, Section 3 of the Regulations (www.opsi.gov.uk/si/si1999/19990293.htm) states:

> **Prohibition on granting planning permission without consideration of environmental information**
>
> 3(2) The relevant planning authority or the Secretary of State or an inspector shall not grant planning permission pursuant to an application to which this regulation applies unless they have first taken the environmental information into consideration, and they shall state in their decision that they have done so.

EIA development is defined as:

> development which is either:
>
> (a) Schedule 1 development; or
> (b) Schedule 2 development likely to have significant effects on the environment by virtue of factors such as its nature, size or location.

Schedules 1 and 2 of the Regulations set out in detail the types of development affected.

Among largely industrial and agricultural categories, Schedule 2 includes infrastructure projects involving industrial estates and urban development projects exceeding 0.5 hectares.

For our purposes, it is the nature of the required assessment that is important. This is set out at Schedule 4 of the regulations and specifically includes the description of the architectural and archaeological heritage affected by such a development, and the assessment of direct, indirect, secondary, cumulative, short-, medium- and long-term, permanent and temporary, positive and negative impacts.

Environmental Impact Assessment (Scotland) Regulations 1999

The Environmental Impact Assessment Regulations in Scotland (www.scotland.gov.uk/library2/doc04/eia-00.htm) make similar provisions, noting:

> 6. The Directive's main aim is to ensure that the authority giving the primary consent (the 'competent authority') for a particular project makes its decision in the knowledge of any likely significant effects on the environment. The Directive therefore sets out a procedure that must be followed for certain types of project before they can be given 'development consent'. This procedure – known as Environmental Impact Assessment (EIA) – is a means of drawing together, in a systematic way, an assessment of a project's likely significant environmental effects. This helps to ensure that the importance of the predicted effects, and the scope for reducing them, are properly understood by the public and the relevant competent authority before it makes its decision.
>
> 7. Projects of the types listed in Annex I to the Directive must always be subject to EIA. Projects of the types listed in Annex II must be subject to EIA whenever they are likely to have significant effects on the environment. A determination of whether or not EIA is required must be made for all projects of a type listed in Annex II.

The relevant project types include:

> **Urban development projects (including the construction of shopping centres and car parks, sports stadiums and multiplex cinemas)**
>
> A18. In addition to the physical scale of such developments, particular consideration should be given to the potential increase in traffic, emissions, and noise. EIA is unlikely to be required for the redevelopment of land unless the new development is on a significantly greater scale than the previous use, or the types of impact are of a markedly different nature or there is a high level of contamination.

A19. Development proposed for sites which have not previously been intensively developed are more likely to require EIA if:

- the site area of the scheme is more than 5 hectares; or
- it would provide a total of more than 10,000 m² of new commercial floorspace; or
- the development would have significant urbanising effects in a previously non-urbanised area (e.g. a new development of more than 1,000 dwellings).

Annex C sets out the information to be provided. This directly corresponds to the Schedule 4 requirements in England and Wales.

Although, within an EIA, the benefits of development in strictly cultural terms can come into consideration with the Cultural Heritage Chapter, built heritage tends to be somewhat isolated from the wider benefits of development. Given the nature of the present national planning guidance, a bespoke Heritage Statement clearly correlating the impact of development on the protected built environment to its wider social and economic benefits can provide a more concise document for making a case for Listed Building or Conservation Area consent.

Ultimately, the importance of establishing the nature of any impacts is to allow the consideration of these within the context of the overall benefits a proposed development will bring.

Chapter 16

Benefits of development

Benefits of development can be considered at two levels:

- cultural benefits
- social and economic benefits.

Cultural benefits

Cultural benefits include the examples of beneficial impacts indicated in the previous chapter:

- the restoration of elements of a Listed Building;
- the improved setting of a Listed Building;
- the enhancement of a Conservation Area.

This can be extended to:

- the cross-funding of restoration projects from new development – enabling development;
- improving local economies in a manner that increases the viability of existing heritage assets and consequently the prospects for their preservation.

The importance of identifying cultural benefits specifically is that they can be seen to directly offset detrimental impacts on heritage assets: that is, if, on balance, the prospects for the preservation or enhancement of the local built heritage is improved by a proposed development, then it can be seen that special regard or attention has been paid to the desirability to preserve or enhance, and so on, as set out in the Planning (Listed Buildings and Conservation Areas) Act.

Exceptional modern design or indeed master-planning of an area should also be considered in this respect. Good, representative modern buildings will become the 'listed buildings' of the future. Consequently, investment in good design must be considered a substantial cultural benefit. In this regard, it is not unusual for a 'trophy' architect to be appointed where the benefit of exceptional design will tip the balance in favour of new development.

Social and economic benefits

Current national planning guidance also directs planning authorities to take into account the potential social and economic benefits of proposed new development. A formal approach to potential social and economic benefits pertaining to specific sites or general locations can be gleaned from any aspirational documents adopted by the local or regional planning authorities, e.g.:

- pertinent local and structure plan policies;
- specific supplementary planning guidance, which might include city-centre action plans, design briefs, conservation management plans and Conservation Area Appraisals.

Typically, such information will identify adopted policies for generating or enhancing retail, business, leisure and residential zones, and perhaps specific policy regarding potential regeneration sites.

This might be extended to include aspirations set out in national policy guidance, such as:

- renewable energy
- tourism
- eco-towns.

Beyond any reference to formally adopted policies, specific demonstrable social and economic benefits identified by the developer are entirely relevant, particularly where no specific supplementary planning guidance has been produced. Benefits to be considered might include:

- local employment
- revitalization
- reconnection
- improved services
- creation of facilities such as museums, schools, health centres, and so on.

Specific benefits offered by the developer that essentially form part of the basis of a planning approval are often formalized under the provisions of the Town and Country Planning Acts (for example, Section 106 Agreements (England and Wales) and Section 75 Agreements (Scotland)).

In decisions pertaining to cases for Listed Building and Conservation Area consent, the balance between the impact of development and the benefits of development is an essential underlying consideration.

Part 3

Case for consent

Introduction

I have found it useful to present cases for Listed Building and/or Conservation Area consent in the form of bespoke Heritage Statements based upon the broad framework of assessments and considerations discussed in Part 2. Such documents should bring together a description of the specific form and aspirations of a proposed development, the relevant statutory requirements and national and local planning policy and guidance upon which the case is to rely, and the objective assessment of significance, impact and benefit, and it should culminate in stating the applicant's justification for consent in all of these terms.

The Heritage Statement is intended to provide the local planning authority, and indeed English Heritage/Historic Scotland, with evidence that the built heritage has been properly considered in accordance with the relevant statutory requirements and national and local planning policy and guidance.

In its final form, the Heritage Statement should not be a document for discussion. The cases made are either to be accepted as the basis for approval by the local planning authority and thereafter the relevant statutory body or, where consent is refused, as the basis of the case that will be made at appeal.

Generally, planning authorities will require some form of 'statement of significance' in relation to any applications involving a Listed Building. Similarly, in larger-scale development proposals, an environmental assessment chapter assessing the impact on cultural heritage of a proposed development will be required. However, such information does not set out a case for consent and leaves control in the hands of the planning authority and other decision-makers to establish if a case can be made. The Heritage Statement is specifically intended to keep the control of the case in the hands of those devising the development proposal.

Chapter 17

Heritage Statement

I have set out below a broad Heritage Statement template that I have used for the presentation of a number of cases for Listed Building and Conservation Area consent.

Introduction and scope

These introductory sections identify the project, the client organization, the basis of the instruction and the qualifications of the person/organization responsible for the production of the document.

Historical background

This section should provide an assessment of the evolution of the development site and its wider local context, as described at Chapter 9 above. This should culminate in a description of the site within its present context and identify any relevant recent planning history.

Heritage assets

All heritage assets that will be affected by the proposed development should be identified in an appropriate order of importance, for example:

- Scheduled Monuments
- Listed Buildings
- Conservation Areas

- World Heritage Sites, and so on
- historic park and gardens/designed landscapes, and so on.

This should be thoroughly researched to ensure that all protected heritage assets are identified.

National and Local Policy and Guidance

The National and Local Policy and Guidance sections should set out the legislation and guidance upon which the justification for consent will rely, in the following general order:

- Acts of Parliament
- national planning guidance
- local planning policy.

It is generally convenient to separate this into two (or more) sections, where the Acts and national guidance provide the global context, and local policy sets out specific local aspirations. All cases should be routed back to the relevant sections of the Acts.

Proposed development

A broad description of the proposed development should be provided, possibly through cross-reference to drawings and design statements submitted in support of the associated application for planning (and Listed Building and/or Conservation Area) consent. It is not the intention of the Heritage Statement to make a detailed assessment of the development proposal. Important considerations are:

- design quality
- impact on heritage assets
- benefits of development.

The specific impact on each and every heritage asset should be identified as a precursor to justification. Such impacts might include:

- demolition of a Listed Building;
- alterations and extensions to a Listed Building;
- changes to the setting of a Listed Building;
- demolition of an unlisted building within a Conservation Area;
- changes to the character and appearance of a Conservation Area.

The Benefits of development should be identified under the headings of:

- cultural benefits
- social and economic benefits.

Individual cases for consent

On the basis of the specific impacts identified and the relevant national and local policy and guidance, provide the detailed justification for consent.

In practice, each heritage asset should be considered in turn, following the general sequence set out below:

- significance of the heritage asset in terms of the Planning (Listed Buildings and Conservation Areas) Acts, for example, the special architectural or historic interest of a Listed Building, the character and appearance of a Conservation Area;
- description of the impact, for example, demolition, alteration;
- correlation of the impact to the benefits to be derived from the development proposal;
- case for consent based on relevant national and local policy and guidance.

Executive summary

A Heritage Statement can become a detailed and bulky technical document. For ease of use in discussions with senior planning officers, planning committee members, etc., an executive summary should be provided that distils the essence of the case being made.

Chapter 18

Cases for consent

Within this section, I have highlighted some of the key principles in relation to the following, typical types of case for Listed Building and Conservation Area consent:

- demolition of a Listed Building;
- alterations and extensions to a Listed Building;
- changes to the setting of a Listed Building;
- demolition of an unlisted building within a Conservation Area;
- changes to the character and appearance of a Conservation Area.

I have included a series of practical examples of cases I have been involved in at Part 4: Case studies.

General

In each instance, the start point is clearly to state the special architectural or historic interest of the Listed Building or its Setting, or the character and appearance of the Conservation Area, and to identify the assessed impact upon that interest. Thereafter, the assessed impact must be correlated to the benefits that will be derived from the proposed change. If no benefit is to be derived from the specific or wider works, on the basis of the special regard or attention that is required to be given to preservation, the impact will not be justifiable.

Demolition of a Listed Building

As discussed in Chapter 6, the justification for the demolition of a Listed Building requires broad consideration under the following general headings:

- importance
- condition
- alternative use
- benefits of redevelopment.

Although the principal justification for demolition more often than not will fall under a single heading, generally assessment under the other headings will be required in mitigation.

Importance

The fact that a building has been listed assumes that it is considered by English Heritage or Historic Scotland to be of special interest. The assessments described in Chapters 11 and 12 will result in a clear understanding of what that special interest is.

It is rarely the case (although not unknown) that a building is listed without a valid reason, or in error. However, in many instances, the building fabric may incorporate alterations or accretions that do not have special architectural or historic interest. The demolition of such additions or accretions should not be considered to affect the special interest of the building and, in some instances, may make what is genuinely important more accessible. In any event, such demolitions will require Listed Building consent.

It may be the case that, subsequent to an early listing, a building has been left to deteriorate or has been altered to such an extent that its original interest has diminished beyond repair. Rather than providing a principle justification for demolition such situations more usually provide mitigation in relation to cases being made under one of the other general headings.

In terms of mitigation, it may be possible to demonstrate that there are other, better local examples of a particular building type or work by the same architect. This in itself could not reasonably be the principal justification for demolition.

Condition

Justification for demolition on the basis of a building's condition will require to be accompanied by a detailed report prepared by a qualified structural engineer. While SHEP, in Scotland, identifies this as a possible singular consideration, it is generally the case that the physical repair of a building, in its own right, is rarely impossible. Consequently, justification on the basis of a Listed Building's condition is generally reliant on factors such as:

- loss of authenticity due to the extent of repairs required (*importance*);
- disproportionate costs of repair when set against the relative importance of the building or its potential for re-use (*importance/alternative use*);
- public health and safety issues (*benefit of redevelopment*).

A structural report can usefully take the form of a separate technical document supporting the case for Listed Building consent. It should provide a consideration of remedial solutions and incorporate or be accompanied by a cost report.

Alternative use

The obvious means to preserve a building whose original use is redundant is to provide it with a sustainable alternative use. Demonstrating that alternative use is not viable provides substantial justification for demolition where there are other mitigating factors.

In most instances, the present local context of a building will be the principal defining factor in establishing relevant alternative uses. Regional and local plans, and adopted supplementary planning guidance and action plans can provide a formal basis for identifying acceptable alternative uses.

However, commercial necessity must be the basis for establishing viability. In this regard, relevant speculative alternative uses can be relatively easily assessed by the use of development appraisals. Such appraisals set the cost of redevelopment against value on the basis of existing accumulated data. Again, this should reflect the existing local context. If the value of the proposed alternative use fails to outstrip the associated costs, then it will be neither viable nor sustainable and will not provide a long-term future for the redundant building.

Consequently, similar to a structural report in relation to condition, the provision of relevant development appraisals is a useful basis for demonstrating the inability to establish viable alternative use as a basis for demolition.

The alternative to the commercial necessity associated with speculative development is the possibility of finding a restoring purchaser with a bespoke interest in the building. This may be in the form of subsidized alternative uses, such as local museums, arts centres, and so on, or a private individual or company, perhaps grant assisted, seeking to adapt the building to its own specific use, for example, a dwelling or a company headquarters.

In this respect, applications for demolition on the basis of the inability to establish a viable alternative use generally require it to be demonstrated that the building has been appropriately marketed. This should be less important where a long planning history demonstrating a failure to find an alternative use is available.

Benefits of redevelopment

As noted at Chapter 8, ultimately it should be considered that the final decision on any application needs to weigh the desirability of preservation against the benefits of any proposed development. In relation to demolition, where there will be a physical loss of historic fabric, derived advantages for the preservation of other more important heritage assets on the site or within the wider area should be highlighted. For example:

- The demolition of a lesser Listed Building element might provide a new build site that will cross-fund the restoration of a more important Listed Building whose preservation would otherwise not be viable.
- The demolition of a lesser building or building element might improve the setting of a more important Listed Building, consequently improving its viability and opportunities for long-term sustainability.

Regarding wider social and economic benefits, the argument will have to be made that the loss of the Listed Building or element is absolutely necessary if the development is to proceed. This is particularly relevant where it has been proven difficult to attract redevelopment or regeneration to a particular area. In this regard it might be argued that the demolition of a lesser building might be absolutely necessary for the creation of a wider development that will improve local economies in a manner that increases the viability of a large number of existing heritage assets and consequently the prospects for their preservation.

It should be considered that, whereas the benefits to be derived from a development are the key generator for the political will and backing required to allow a major project to proceed, where the demolition of a Listed Building or Buildings is necessary, substantial mitigation, if not justification, under the other headings indicated above, will be pivotal to maintaining such support. Consequently, it is unlikely that the social and economic benefits of development could successfully be the sole justification for the demolition of a Listed Building.

Alteration and extension to a Listed Building

Making the case for the alteration of a Listed Building is similar to making a case for demolition. However, where the Listed Building is essentially to be retained, it is the minimization of the necessary impact upon its special interest, set against the benefits to be gained from the proposed alterations, that is the decisive consideration.

Importance

The detailed assessment of the special architectural and/or historic interest of the building is critical to establishing the significance of any impact.

It is important to ascertain the overall history of the building and the most significant periods in its evolution. In many instances, a building's importance may not be restricted to its original form. A Georgian building may have been substantially remodelled during the later Victorian period, with the works from both periods being of special interest.

As a general rule, additions or alterations to a Listed Building should be subservient to the special interest of the building. Where the alteration or extension to the building requires the addition of a specific new entity, modern design is more often than not considered preferable to pastiche.

Assessment will also identify elements of lesser importance and utilitarian accretions that are of no significance or indeed detract from the special interest of the building.

It should be noted that, under Section 1(5), in England and Wales, and Section 1(4) in Scotland, of the Planning (Listed Buildings and Conservation Areas) Acts, accretions are considered to be part of the Listed Building, and their removal requires Listed Building consent. However, the removal of such accretions is an example of where alterations might be justified on the basis of importance alone.

Condition

As with demolition, justification for the removal of elements of a Listed Building on the basis of its poor structural condition should be accompanied by a structural report. Any substantial removal of significant building elements will tend toward demolition and will have to be justified in those terms. In this respect, façade retention should properly be considered under the provisions for demolition, the retained façade being promoted as a considerable mitigating factor (that is, the alternative to complete demolition).

Alternative use

The long-term future use of a Listed Building may require its conversion to an alternative use. Demonstrating the appropriateness of various alternative uses is again best presented in the form of development appraisals, where viability can be relatively easily demonstrated.

Establishing a building in an alternative use, in most cases, will require it to be upgraded to meet current building regulations and health and safety standards. In this regard, substantial alterations that might be justified on the basis of maintaining a Listed Building in a viable alternative use include:

- fire-escape provision
- fire separation
- disabled access
- thermal and sound insulation
- floor-loading capacity
- services installations
- security.

In each instance, the basis for such alterations will require to be identified and demonstrated.

Subdivision of internal spaces is a particular issue in relation to the alteration of Listed Buildings. Where subdivision is necessary, the principle of reversibility might be cited in mitigation (that is, that the alterations are not such that the space could not be returned to its existing form).

Benefits of redevelopment

In terms of cultural benefits, the central justification for the alteration of a Listed Building is that it will be provided with a sustainable, long-term future. However, it is also clear that the regeneration of a single deteriorating or redundant Listed Building may revitalize a local area such that it will directly improve the prospects for the long-term preservation of the wider local heritage.

Beyond this, the social and economic benefits should be considered in mitigation in the same manner as for an application for demolition.

Changes to the setting of a Listed Building

It is important to note that, although setting is not a matter for Listed Building consent, as such, it is very often a principal means of justifying the refusal of planning consent and should be given careful consideration at the outset.

Applications for planning consent that will affect the setting of a Listed Building should be accompanied by a statement that addresses this issue. In marginal cases, this may be best dealt with in the architect's design statement, where it can be discussed among the various other design criteria taken into account by the applicant. Where it is a clear individual issue, or is related to issues that require Listed Building or Conservation Area consent, it is better highlighted within a Heritage Statement where it can be seen to have been considered in detail.

Two essential bases for justifying changes to the setting of a Listed Building are that the change will improve the setting of the building or, in more neutral circumstances, that the associated social and economic benefits to be derived from the change will outweigh its physical impact.

Of the former, examples include:

- the replacement of a utilitarian setting that has accrued over a period of time with a setting specifically designed to accentuate the special interest of the Listed Building;
- the removal of utilitarian elements in order to return a historically more appropriate setting – where the assessment of the evolution of the local area becomes important.

Justification of impact on the basis of the social and economic benefits of development should be presented on the same mitigating basis as for the demolition or alteration of a Listed Building.

Demolition of an unlisted building within a Conservation Area

Making a case for the demolition of an unlisted building within a Conservation Area is similar to that for the demolition of a Listed Building. However, the central issue is the unlisted building's importance in terms of its contribution to the character and appearance of the Conservation Area. In this respect, very much more reliance can be placed on importance as a principal justification for demolition.

Where assessment concludes that the unlisted building does contribute to the character of a Conservation Area, then condition, alternative use and the benefits of development become more significant considerations.

Where justification for the demolition of a building of some character can be made under one or all of these other headings, the retention of the façade or external features of the building might be considered a means of minimizing the effect on the Conservation Area.

Changes to the character and appearance of a Conservation Area

Like change affecting the setting of a Listed Building, change to the character and appearance of a Conservation Area is not a matter for Conservation Area consent. However, it is very often cited as a principal basis for justifying the refusal of planning consent.

Where the character and appearance of the area will not be preserved, then the extent to which any proposed change will reflect a desirability to enhance the Conservation Area is required to be given special attention.

In this regard, the case requires to be made, in the first instance, on the basis of published aspirations. These can be supplemented or, where they do not exist, be based upon further considerations such as:

- improving the vibrancy and vitality of an area;
- improving infrastructure;
- improving the interconnection and accessibility of an area;
- removing utilitarian built elements that detract from the character and appearance of an area.

General

The principal aim of presenting a case for Listed Building or Conservation Area consent, or a statement in relation to other conservation matters is to provide an as objective as possible justification in terms of the prevailing planning acts, policy and guidance. This in itself cannot be a conclusive process; it can only, at best, direct decision-makers toward understanding that consent can be given in such terms. Outwith the actual mechanics of making the case for consent, the wider strategy for successfully maximizing any development goals requires:

- the developer to lead the process based upon a full understanding of the controlling principles. Whereas a proposal will inevitably evolve through discussion with a planning authority, the defining point will be where no further compromise can be given – i.e., where the development is no longer viable on the developer's terms;
- the developer actively to maintain contact with those ultimately responsible for decision-making at the highest relevant level. It should be acknowledged that, as the benefits that will be derived from major development are generally the tipping point, the final decision is always, ultimately, political.

Chapter 19

Design

Although architectural design cannot in itself justify the loss of a Listed Building or any other substantial impact upon a protected heritage asset, design is a material planning consideration, and the pursuit of an exceptional design can be taken to be a further mitigating factor where a significant impact is inevitable. In this regard, the careful selection of a specifically experienced architect or master planner can be seen to demonstrate a developer's commitment to addressing particular issues.

Design should not be considered in isolation from the heritage case; rather, it should inform and be informed by it. The most difficult cases to make at appeal are those that have had a post-rationalized heritage case applied after the event. Heritage assessment should be undertaken either by the architect or an appointed specialist consultant as part of establishing the essential design parameters for the project site.

CABE, in England and Wales, and A&DS, in Scotland, are the principal publicly appointed statutory consultees regarding architectural design and where major development is proposed should be approached as soon as the initial design development has been sufficiently progressed. Many local authorities also appoint in-house advisors in design matters.

Similar to conservation issues, the developer must lead on the issue of design. Both CABE and AD&S are populated by many good design architects, with many diverse views but with limited time or opportunity to investigate in detail the full breadth of the design parameters driving any particular proposal. In this regard, their comments are often of a superficial nature that can be robustly countered by a detailed understanding of the design issues affecting a site.

The use of national policy documents on design matters can superimpose some level of objectivity on design. Relevant publications can be found at:

- in England and Wales: www.cabe.org.uk/publications;
- in Scotland: www.ads.org.uk/about/corporate_publications.

Most important, in terms of making an application for planning consent involving Listed Buildings and/or Conservation Area matters, is the quality of supporting visual information. The accurate representation of the impact that any development will have on an existing historic environment is essential to both the assessment of that impact and to the presentation of the development proposal in its best light.

Besides the plans, sections and elevations normally submitted with any planning application, proposals might usefully be supported by:

- wireframe diagrams and photomontages demonstrating 'before and after' views from principal viewpoints; these can be agreed with the local authority and/or English Heritage or Historic Scotland;
- physical models with interchangeable 'before and after' elements;
- computer models providing 360° views and 'fly throughs'.

It should be remembered that, not only will these visual representations be seen to enable the assessment of impact, they will also be essential to attracting support and presenting the proposals.

Part 4

Case studies

Introduction

Within this part of the book, I have included three case studies relating to successful applications for Listed Building Consent that I have been directly involved in over the past few years. Although the relevant specific national guidance is generally that relating to Scotland (and in some cases has since been superseded), as set out in the previous parts of this book, the principles adopted are rooted in the Planning (Listed Buildings and Conservation Areas) Act 1990 and the Planning (Listed Buildings and Conservation Areas) (Scotland) Act 1997, whose essential provisions are interchangeable.

The Heritage Statements referred to are all in the public domain and can generally be accessed in full through the relevant local authority planning portals.

Other substantial applications that reflect the methodology set out in this book, and should be available through relevant planning portals, include:

- Quartermile, the former Royal Infirmary of Edinburgh;
- Regeneration proposal for the south side of St Andrew Square, Edinburgh;
- Forthquarter, the former Granton Gasworks.

Case Study 1

Caltongate, Edinburgh

Introduction

Caltongate is a redevelopment proposal for the semi-derelict hinterland on the northern slope of the Canongate in the heart of the Old and New Towns of Edinburgh World Heritage Site. It integrates what was historically an industrialized backland into the wider fabric of the city by creating physical connections with the Canongate, Waverley Railway Station and Princes Street beyond (Figures 1.1 and 1.2).

1.2
Photomontage of approved scheme (courtesy of Allan Murray Architects)

Statutory consent for the proposal was achieved in two stages. First, a master plan for the area was developed in association with the local authority. This was adopted in October 2006 and thereafter provided a specific policy background against which a series of detailed applications for Planning, Listed Building and Conservation Area consent were submitted in 2007. These were approved by the City of Edinburgh Council in late 2007 and effectively fully approved in June 2008, when it was confirmed that, as the constituent parts of a major application, they were not going to be 'called in' by the Scottish Government.

The Heritage Statement setting out the associated cases for Listed Building and Conservation Area consent was a substantial document. In this regard, I have summarized the findings of the underlying assessment and only quoted directly from the document in relation to selected representative aspects of the case that was made.

The full document can be accessed on the City of Edinburgh Council Planning Portal at http://citydev-portal.edinburgh.gov.uk/portal/submissions.do?action=View PublicCaseDetails&applicationRef=07/01237/FUL.

Site

The development site originally comprised the former New Street Bus Garage site but was expanded to include: 231 Canongate (Old Sailor's Ark), 221–229 Canongate, the former School Building at 5 New Street (the Canongate Venture), East Market Street and various packages of land on the south side of Market Street, including the disused arches under Jeffrey Street, and various packages of land on Calton Road (see Figures 1.1 and 1.2).

Development proposal

The key elements of the proposed development were:

- new square connecting with Canongate, East Market Street (and Waverley Station and Princes Street beyond) and Calton Hill (see Figure 1.3);
- five-star hotel with principal façades on Canongate and the north side of the new square (Figures 1.3 and 1.4);
- office building extending from the south side of the new square to Calton Road (Figures 1.3 and 1.5);
- residential flatted accommodation extending from Canongate to Calton Road and overlooking the eastern side of the new square (Figure 1.5);
- redevelopment of East Market Street and the vaulted arches below Jeffrey Street (Figures 1.6 and 1.7);
- landmark building located on Jeffrey Street, overlooking the Waverley valley (Figure 1.8).

All of which required to be considered in terms of the benefits and impact that they would have on the cultural heritage of the development site and the surrounding areas.

1.3
Perspective of approved square looking toward East Market Street (courtesy of Allan Murray Architects)

1.4
Perspective of approved scheme looking toward Old Sailor's Ark (courtesy of Allan Murray Architects)

1.5
Perspective of approved scheme looking toward railway bridge on Calton Road (courtesy of Allan Murray Architects)

1.6
View toward Caltongate site along East Market Street (courtesy of Allan Murray Architects)

1.7
View up Cranston Street from East Market Street (courtesy of Allan Murray Architects)

1.8
**Perspective of
approved scheme
from Jeffrey Street
(courtesy of Allan
Murray Architects)**

Heritage Statement

Substantial Heritage Statements were prepared in support of both the master plan in the first instance and thereafter as an umbrella document for the various detailed applications that followed. The following summaries and extracts are based on the umbrella Heritage Statement that accompanied the applications for detailed planning consent.

National and local policy and guidance

The following underlying statutory requirements and specific national and local policy and guidance were identified as the basis of the overall assessment. In this instance the then relevant key national guidance was that set out in NPPG 18 and the Memorandum of Guidance, the predecessors to SPP 23 and SHEP:

- Planning (Listed Buildings and Conservation Areas) (Scotland) Act 1997;
- NPPG 18: Planning and the Historic Environment;
- the Memorandum of Guidance on Listed Buildings and Conservation Areas (1998);

- Old Town Conservation Area character appraisal;
- the Old and New Towns of Edinburgh World Heritage Site Management Plan (2005);
- New Town Conservation Area character appraisal;
- the Waverley Valley redevelopment strategy;
- Edinburgh and the Lothians structure plan 2015 (2004);
- Central Edinburgh local plan (1997 – reviewed 2000);
- emerging Edinburgh City local plan;
- World Heritage Site Convention;
- World Heritage Site Manifesto;
- passed to the Future (Historic Scotland 2002).

After its adoption in October 2006, the Caltongate master plan became a relevant principal specific policy document.

Historical background

The historical background to the site and surrounding area was principally assessed against an analysis of historical plans and OS maps sourced from the National Map Library, including:

- James Gordon's Perspective of City of Edinburgh, published *c.*1650 (Figures 1.9a and b);
- James Gordon's Plan, Edinodunensis Tabulam, published *c.*1650 (Figure 1.10);
- the Kincaid Plan, published in 1784 (Figure 1.11);
- Kirkwood's Plan, published in 1821 (Figure 1.12);
- Revised plan of projected improvements of the Old Town of Edinburgh (Cousin & Lessels), published November 1866 (Figure 1.13)
- OS maps, 1896, 1914, 1931, 1948, 1971, 1980 to present (Figures 1.14 and 1.15).

The critical development periods were assessed under the following broad headings:

- early/medieval burghs (up to mid eighteenth century);
- expansion of Edinburgh (from mid eighteenth to mid nineteenth century);
- Edinburgh Improvement Acts (mid to late nineteenth century);
- decline in Canongate's status (1800–1980);
- conservation (1900–1980);
- regeneration (1980s onwards).

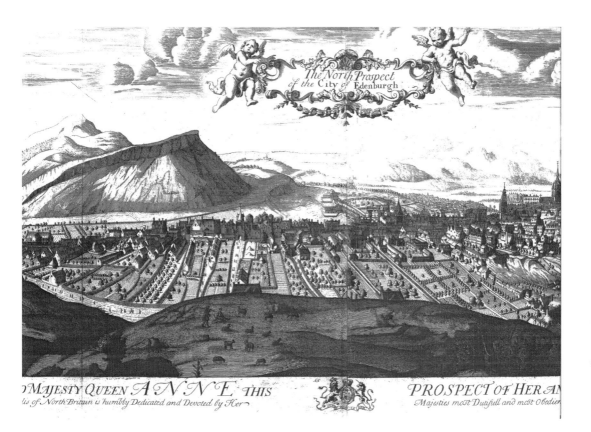

The North Prospect of the City of Edinburgh

..O MAJESTY QUEEN *ANNE* THIS ... PROSPECT OF HER A...
...ls of North Britain is humbly Dedicated and Devoted by Her— ... Majesties most Dutifull and most Obedie...

1.9a and b

Extract and close up from James Gordon's Perspective of City of Edinburgh, *c.*1650. Reproduced by permission of the Trustees of the National Library of Scotland

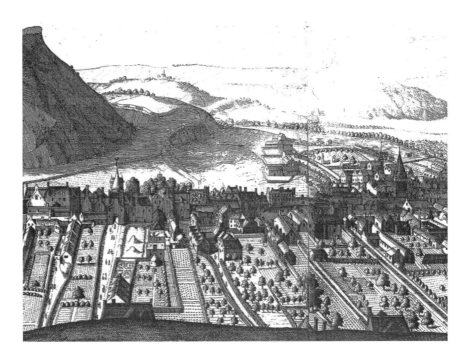

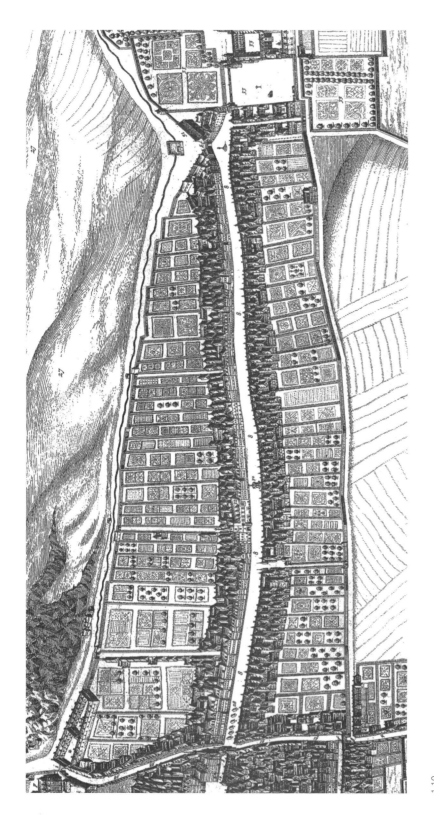

1.10

Close-up of extract from James Gordon's plan, Edinodunensis Tabulam, c.1650. Reproduced by permission of the Trustees of the National Library of Scotland

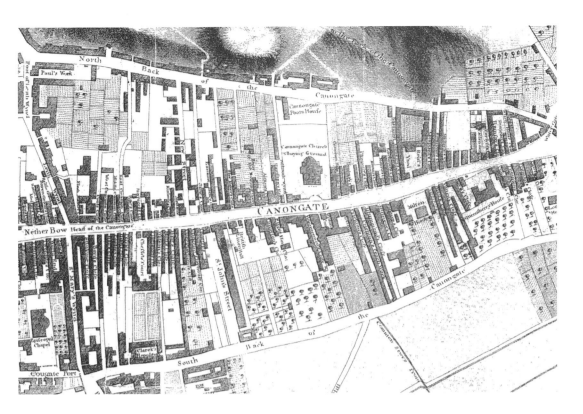

1.11
**Close-up from
1784 Kincaid Plan.
Reproduced by
permission of the
Trustees of the
National Library
of Scotland**

1.12
**Extract from 1821 Kirkwood Plan. Reproduced by permission of the Trustees of the National Library
of Scotland**

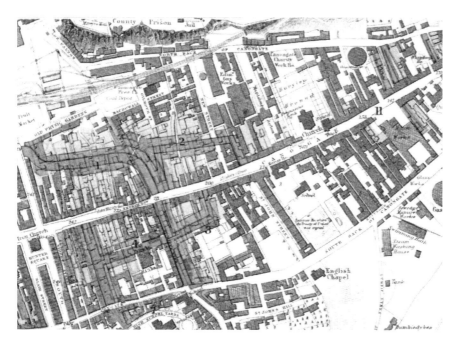

1.13
Revised plan
of projected
improvements
of the Old Town of
Edinburgh (Cousin &
Lessels), published
November 1866.
Reproduced by
permission of the
Trustees of the
National Library of
Scotland

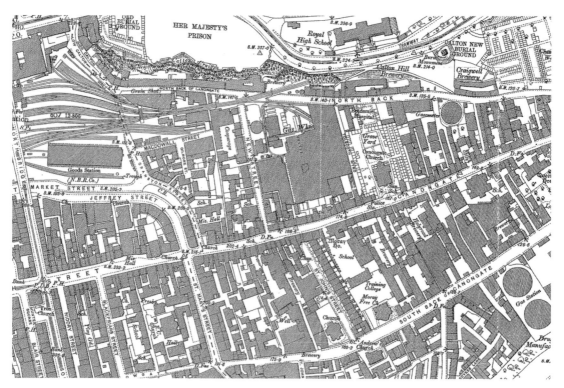

1.14
Close-up from 1896 OS map. Reproduced by permission of the Trustees of the National Library
of Scotland

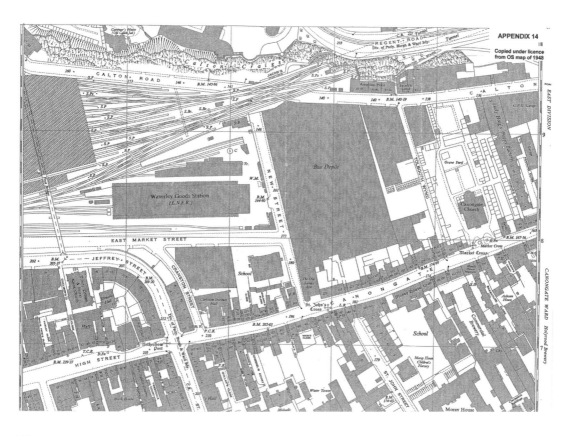

1.15
**Extract from 1948
OS map. Reproduced
by permission of the
Trustees of the
National Library of
Scotland**

1.16
**View up Canongate
(courtesy of Allan
Murray Architects)**

1.17
View up Tolbooth
Wynd from Calton
Road (courtesy of
Allan Murray
Architects)

1.18
View east along
Calton Road
(courtesy of Allan
Murray Architects)

1.19
Listed Buildings,
Caltongate © Crown
Copyright and/or
database right. All
rights reserved.
Licence number
100049743

Identification of heritage assets

Thereafter, the various heritage assets that would be impacted upon by the development proposals were established using the Pastmap website and the Local Plan (Figure 1.19).

Listed Buildings

As the development proposals evolved, it was considered that they would potentially have a direct impact on four Listed Buildings located within or immediately adjacent the development site:

Listed Building/structure	Listing category
231 Canongate (Old Sailor's Ark)	Category C(S) Listed
5 New Street (the Canongate Venture)	Category C(S) Listed
Jeffrey Street, wall, vaults, railings and pier	Category C(S) Listed
4–18 Jeffrey Street and 3–9 Cranston Street	Category B Listed

It was also assessed that it would have a perceivable impact on the setting of over twenty other Listed Buildings in areas adjacent to the site:

Listed Building/structure	Listing category
Royal High School, Regent Road	Category A Listed
St Andrew's House, Regent Road	Category A Listed
Governor's House (formerly of Calton Jail)	Category A Listed
Regent Road retaining wall	Category B Listed
Monuments on Calton Hill	Category A Listed
Calton Old Burying Ground and Monuments	Category A Listed
Canongate Parish Church	Category A Listed
Canongate Parish Church Churchyard	Category B Listed
167–169 Canongate (Tollbooth Tavern)	Category A Listed
183–187 Canongate (Bible Land)	Category B Listed
189 – 191 Canongate (Flats 2, 4 and 6)	Category B Listed
191 Canongate (Flats 1, 3 and 5)	Category B Listed
195–197 Canongate (Shoemaker's Land)	Category B Listed
249–263 Canongate and 43 New Street (Morocco Land)	Category B Listed
265–267 Canongate (Morocco Land)	Category B Listed
271 Canongate (former Canongate United Presbyterian Church)	Category C(S) Listed
174 Canongate (Moray House)	Category A Listed
176–184 Canongate	Category C(S) Listed

continued . . .

. . . continued

Listed Building/structure	Listing category
194–198 Canongate (Old Playhouse Close)	Category B Listed
3–37 Jeffrey Street	Category B Listed
4–18 Jeffrey Street and 3–9 Cranston Street	Category B Listed
Jeffrey Street, wall, vaults, railings and pier	Category C(S) Listed
2 Cranston Street (former Canongate Christian Institute)	Category C(S) Listed

Conservation Areas

The site was located almost entirely within the north-eastern part of the Old Town Conservation Area and immediately adjacent the south-eastern part of the New Town Conservation Area (a small part was located within the New Town Conservation Area).

In this respect, it was recognized that the development would potentially have an impact on the character and appearance of both Conservation Areas and a direct impact on the following unlisted buildings within the Old Town Conservation Area:

- 221–223 Canongate
- 227–229 Canongate
- Car depot, East Market Street
- 20 Calton Road
- Calton Hill Stairs.

Other designations

The proposed development was wholly located within the Old and New Towns of Edinburgh World Heritage Site.

It was also established that a small part of the site was technically located within the New Town Gardens area included within Historic Scotland's inventory of gardens and designed landscapes, although, in the event, no significant impacts were identified in this respect.

Benefits and impacts

The specific envisaged benefits and impacts of the proposed development were set out as a precursor to developing the cases for Listed Building and Conservation Area consent that formed the latter part of the assessment.

Benefits

In terms of the relevant policy, the advantages for development were to be considered in terms of social and economic benefits. In relation to the master plan submission, the Heritage Assessment used the stated aspirations of the adopted Waverley Valley Redevelopment Strategy as the principal basis for identifying the recognizable benefits that would accrue from the master plan proposal. Within the Heritage Assessment accompanying the subsequent detailed planning and Listed Building consent submissions, the adopted master plan became the key indicator. In this respect, the key benefits indentified therein were:

- to bring increased population, related local services and a mix of uses to the area;
- to create new streets and spaces that establish new urban connections through the Valley, which will encourage ease of movement and generate activity within the Old Town by increasing frontage and unlocking the potential of development sites;
- to create a major new public square – fitting in with a growing family of public spaces off the Royal Mile – offering the means to regenerate Canongate and bring an additional focus and destination;
- to create new buildings and spaces of the highest architectural and urban design quality that conserve and reinforce the existing historic and landscape context.

In terms of these aspirations within the accompanying Heritage Statement, the social, economic and cultural benefits that were to be derived from the Caltongate Development Project were identified as follows:

a) To bring increased population, related local services and a mix of uses to the area.

The Caltongate Development Project will bring the following uses into the area:

- open market housing
- affordable housing
- community facilities
- offices
- affordable business units
- retail
- cafes
- five-star hotel and conference centre.

The introduction of this significant mix of uses will generate an increased permanent and transitory population.

b) To create new streets and spaces that establish new urban connections through the Valley that will encourage ease of movement and generate activity within the Old Town by increasing frontage and unlocking the potential of development sites.

The principal driver for the Caltongate Development Project from the outset has been to reconnect re-emerging Canongate/Holyrood to the wider city, using the necessary regeneration of the former Bus Garage site and other derelict and under-used sites on East Market Street and Calton Road as the catalyst.

The creation of a clearly defined principal pedestrian route of easy gradient from Waverley to the Canongate is an essential element that will attract people into, and activate, the new district. Thereafter existing, and new, streets and wynds will ensure the permeability of the area. Existing connections across the valley will be redefined and added to.

The activation of East Market Street will unlock the development potential of the presently unused Jeffrey Street Vaults. The redevelopment of the south side of East Market Street from Cranston Street to New Street addresses an essential requirement to activate what is presently a sterile and uninviting street frontage.

The interaction of the new district with Canongate and Waverley are critical to the success of the Project. In this regard the physical connection onto the Canongate, the creation of a five star hotel and conference centre with a Canongate frontage, and the activation of East Market Street are fundamental components.

c) To create a major new public square – fitting in with a growing family of public spaces off the Royal Mile – offering the means to regenerate Canongate and bring an additional focus and destination.
The proposed new public square off the Royal Mile is the essential focus of the development. It creates a central public space from which all of the principle commercial elements of the Project, the five-star hotel and conference centre, the office complex and retail spaces are accessed. It provides a nodal destination for pedestrian routes to and from Calton Hill, Waverley Station and beyond and through the Old Town.

The physical connection between the new square and Canongate is essential to ensuring the activation of this space and the commercial viability of all of the functions it supports.

d) To create new buildings and spaces of the highest architectural and urban design quality that conserve and reinforce the existing historic and landscape context.
The developer is committed to creating new buildings and a new urban infrastructure of the highest architectural quality. In this respect five separate award winning architectural practices are involved.

A detailed assessment of the existing historic and landscape context, in order to establish the key characteristics and to establish the parameters within which change can be made, has from the outset been the essential basis for the design of the master plan and the detailed design of the individual component buildings.

The sensitive regeneration of this extensive area of derelict land and buildings at the heart of Old Town will make a dynamic and positive contribution to its contemporary use and its sustainable future.

It is recognised that a localised physical impact upon the existing built fabric will be necessary to enable the Caltongate Development Project to proceed.

Underlying all of the above benefits will be the creation of a viable new district that is properly integrated into the fabric of the wider city and, notwithstanding necessary localised interventions, properly respects and enhances its historic context.

In order to address the identifiable cultural impacts on the existing built heritage, a list of specific cultural or heritage benefits associated with the proposals was included:

Specific Cultural or Heritage Benefits
In broad terms the specific cultural or heritage benefits associated with the implementation of the Caltongate master plan in the manner proposed under the Caltongate Development Project are:

a) The enhancement of the character and appearance of the Old Town Conservation Area and the Old and New Towns of Edinburgh World Heritage Site by regenerating a significant, presently semi-derelict part of these areas.

b) The proper re-connection of the re-emerging Canongate and Holyrood with the wider city (Figures 1.21 and 1.22).

c) The re-vitalisation of the Canongate, by the introduction of new uses that will activate the street, and the consequent enhancement of its character and appearance as part of the Royal Mile.

d) The development of the Category C(S) Listed Jeffrey Street Arches in sustainable use, on the basis of their interrelationship with the new district.

e) The replacement of existing utilitarian piecemeal development along East Market Street with a specifically integrated urban street, with all the opportunities this creates for new 'traditional' connections between the Canongate and Market Street, in the form of wynds and closes.

f) The improved sightlines and connectivity between the Canongate and Calton Hill, including new or improved framed views towards the monuments on Calton Hill, and consequently the improved presentation of the historic built environment in these areas.

g) The improved prospects for the maintenance of the existing historic built fabric on the basis of the improved economic environment.

h) Specifically, the improved prospects for the sustainable ongoing use of Category B Listed Milton House Primary School on the Canongate.

1.20
Proposed location of the breakthrough to the Canongate at Big Jack's Close (courtesy of Allan Murray Architects)

1.21
Perspective of approved breakthrough (courtesy of Allan Murray Architects)

i)   The improved prospects for the further sympathetic regeneration of the Canongate between the Canongate Parish Church and Holyrood. This is an area where a number of distinctly dreary utilitarian buildings have been introduced in the late 20th century.

k)   The reintroduction of traditional paving and other materials under the public realm improvements proposed.

Impacts

Against this, the recognized impacts on the existing built heritage were identified as:

A. Impact on Listed Buildings

a)   The partial demolition of the Category C(S) Listed Old Sailors Ark.

b)   The demolition of the Category C(S) Listed Canongate Venture (5 New Street).

c)   The alterations to the Category C(S) Listed wall, vaults, railings and pier at Jeffrey Street.

d)   The minor alterations to the Category B Listed north gable wall of 12–18 Jeffrey Street and 7–9 Cranston Street.

e)   The impacts on the settings of various Listed Buildings and Structures on the Canongate, Jeffrey Street, Regent's Road and Calton Hill, adjacent the master plan area.

B. Impact on Conservation Area

f)   The demolition with part retained façades of unlisted 1930s tenements (221–229 Canongate) to enable the connection of 'Parliament Way' into the Canongate, and the creation of a new five star hotel on the Canongate.

g)   The demolition of the former Car Depot in East Market Street, in order to bring otherwise 'sterilised' runs of Market Street and New Street frontage into viable street level use.

h)   The demolition of 20 Calton Road.

i)   The impacts upon what are considered to be the essential characteristics of the Old Town Conservation Area.

C. Impact on World Heritage Site

j)   The impacts upon what are considered to be the features of universal value within the Old and New Towns of Edinburgh World Heritage Site.

In setting out the benefits and impacts in this manner, it was intended to provide a straightforward set of parameters against which the essential cases for Listed Building and Conservation Area consent would be set and upon which a decision would eventually require to be based.

Essential components

In a subsequent section of the Heritage Statement, the essential components for the development, without which it would not be viable, were stated thus:

Introduction

The economic and architectural feasibility of the Caltongate Development Project is reliant upon the following essential components that must be considered in relation to their localised impact upon the existing built fabric. These are:

- The Connection into the Canongate.
- The specific provision of a Five-Star Hotel and Conference Centre.
- The activation of East Market Street . . .

These essential requirements were set against the acknowledged impact on a number of Listed Buildings and unlisted buildings within the Old Town Conservation Area:

Cases for Listed Building and Conservation Area Consent

That the benefits to be derived from the wider development are dependent upon these is the essential basis for the individual cases for Listed Building and Conservation Area Consent for:

- The partial demolition of the Category C(S) Listed Old Sailors Ark.
- The demolition of the Category C(S) Listed Canongate Venture (5 New Street).
- The alterations to the Category C(S) Listed Vaults below Jeffrey Street to various uses as workshops and artist studios.
- The minor alterations to the Category B Listed north gable wall of 12–18 Jeffrey Street and 7–9 Cranston Street.
- The demolition, with part retained façades, of unlisted 1930s tenements (221–229 Canongate).
- The demolition of the former Car Depot in East Market Street . . .

This section concluded:

Conclusions

. . . It is acknowledged that these essential component parts are the aspects of the project that will have the most significant localised impacts upon the existing built heritage.

In this regard, in terms set out within NPPG 18 and the Memorandum of Guidance, it is incumbent upon the City of Edinburgh Council to make a reasonable judgement as to whether the benefits of the proposed development, which are reliant upon these essential components, will outweigh their localised impact. The Caltongate master plan in the form adopted signals that, in principle, the Council accept that this is the case and that it is the detailed design of these (and the other elements making up the entire project) that requires final scrutiny.

In mitigation, in each instance, the detailed design of these essential components seeks to minimise the acknowledged impacts on the existing built heritage and has responded to comments made during an extensive consultation process.

In an acknowledged need to provide diversity over what was a large site, six separate architectural practices, Allan Murray Architects (the architect for the master plan), Comprehensive Design Architects, RHWL, Page & Park, Malcolm Fraser and Zone Architects, were involved in the detail design of the various component elements of the development proposal. Each practice submitted a design statement as part of its submissions. These were cross-referenced and summarized within the Heritage Statement.

All of the above information set the background against which the cases for Listed Building and Conservation Area consent and the assessment of the impact on the Conservation Areas and World Heritage Site could be made.

Cases for consent

For the purposes of brevity, I have referred only to the following cases made in relation to the various applications:

- Listed Building consent for the partial demolition of the Old Sailor's Ark;
- the Setting of Listed Buildings;
- the preservation or enhancement of the Old Town Conservation Area.

Listed Building consent for the partial demolition of the Old Sailor's Ark

I have included below, in full with comments, the section of the Heritage Statement setting out the case for Listed Building consent for the partial demolition of the Old Sailor's Ark:

Impact on Listed Buildings: The Old Sailor's Ark

Introduction

Within this section the proposed partial demolition of the Old Sailor's Ark is discussed in terms of the tests set out in NPPG 18 and the Memorandum of Guidance and the Caltongate master plan.

In this regard, the then applicable guidance was that which preceded the current guidance set out in SPP 23 and SHEP and more specifically considered justification for demolition under the following headings:

- importance
- condition

- alternative uses
- benefits of development.

Importance

The importance of the Listed Building was assessed as follows:

Importance

The Old Sailor's Ark was Category C(S) Listed on 1 February 2000. Within the Memorandum of Guidance Category C(S) Listing is defined as:

> . . . buildings of local importance, lesser examples of any period, style or building type, as originally constructed or altered, and simple, traditional buildings, which group well with categories A and B or are part of a plan group such as an estate or industrial complex.

In terms of the principles of Listing set out within the Memorandum of Guidance the following principles would appear to apply:

> c. Buildings erected between 1914 and 1945 are listed if they are good examples of the works of an important Architect, or of a particular style, whether it be traditional, progressive or international modern . . .
>
> i   The works of better-known Architects.
>
> iv   Distinctive regional variations in design and use of materials.

The Information Supplementary to the Statutory List, published by Historic Scotland, describes the Old Sailor's Ark as follows:

> Tarbolton & Ochterlony, 1934–6. 4-storey, 5-bay Hostel, with 17th century detailing and flat roof. Rubble-jointed sandstone, with polished ashlar dressings. Base course; eaves course . . .
>
> S (PRINCIPAL) ELEVATION: 5-bay, comprising advanced single bay 4-storey tower with curved corners, to outer left, remainder of elevation symmetrical, comprising advanced doorpiece centred at ground, with pilasters flanking doorway, with corniced frieze at impost level, keystone motif, pair of sliding studded vertically boarded timber doors, tripartite 2-leaf glazed rectilinear pattern glazed inner doors . . . (Figures 1.23, 1.24 and 1.25).
>
> W (NEW STREET) ELEVATION: 9-bay, on falling ground to N, grouped 3, 6; 3-bay section to right comprising windows in bays at ground, windows in central bay and bay to left at 1st and 2nd floors, windows in bays at 3rd floor; red brick recessed remainder of elevation comprising timber door with 8-pane rectangular fanlight . . . (Figures 1.25 and 1.26).

1.22

**View down Canongate
from Old Sailor's Ark
(courtesy of Allan
Murray Architects)**

1.23

**Old Sailor's Ark from
Canongate (courtesy
of Hurd Rolland
Partnership)**

1.24
**Old Sailor's Ark
entrance screen
(courtesy of Hurd
Rolland Partnership)**

1.25
**View down New Street toward Calton Hill from
Canongate (courtesy of Allan Murray Architects)**

1.26
Scaffolding to rear part of Old Sailor's Ark (courtesy of Hurd Rolland Partnership)

1.27
Rear part of Old Sailor's Ark from Gladstone's Land (courtesy of Allan Murray Architects)

1.29
Old Sailor's Ark stairwell (courtesy of Hurd Rolland Partnership)

1.30
Old Sailor's Ark:
water ingress
damage (courtesy
of Hurd Rolland
Partnership)

1.31
Interior of rear part
of Old Sailor's Ark
(courtesy of Hurd
Rolland Partnership)

1.32
**Perspective of
approved scheme
down New Street
toward Calton Hill
(courtesy of Allan
Murray Architects)**

E ELEVATION: obscured by adjoining building at street. 6-bay rear elevation to New Street red brick block with irregular fenestration, including 3-storey stylised oriel windows corbelled out at 1st floor in bays 2nd, 3rd and 4th from right, with windows at both floors (Figure 1.27).

Predominantly multi-pane timber sash and case windows, predominantly casement windows to New Street Block. Flat roof, not seen, 1999. Cast-iron rainwater goods, including hopper dated '1936'.

INTERIOR: includes contemporary rectilinear-patterned glazed doors . . . (Figures 1.24 and 1.28–1.31).

The supplementary information concludes by noting:

An unusual combination of 17th Century detailing and rubble stonework to principal elevation, modern flat roof and brick rear.

Tarbolton & Ochterlony were relatively well-known architects, local to Edinburgh, and in this respect the Old Sailor's Ark can be considered the work of a better-known architect. In accordance with its Category C(S) Listing, the importance of the building is recognized to be of a local nature.

The building was constructed on the site of Kames House and an earlier tenement located immediately in front of it on the Canongate, in the early 1930s, during the period of the regeneration initiative pursued by the City Architect, E. J. McRae. Although it uses materials similar to that of the two tenement buildings by McRae at 221–229 Canongate (but in a much more random pattern (see Figures 1.22 and 1.23)), it makes no attempt to replicate the tenemental style of the Canongate. Indeed, although elements of the detailing may be considered seventeenth century, its overall style is distinctly art deco.

Its main entrance façade is set back from the Canongate building line, suggesting that it is a building of some importance (in line with its 'Scottish baronial' pretensions). That it is not a building with any significant use (with the exception of the basement, it is presently not in use) makes this semi-private space somewhat incongruous at this location and ultimately merely adds to the failure of the street frontage to interact with the street.

In appearance and plan form, the Ark is a building of two parts. The rear is of brick-clad, concrete frame construction and of an uncompromising modern appearance tending towards art deco in style (Figure 1.27). At the part of the building fronting onto Canongate and returning into New Street, the essentially art deco nature of the overall design has been adapted to incorporate a level of historical detailing, and materials have been altered to reflect those used in the replicated tenements designed by McRae (Figure 1.23). It is probable that these inclusions were a compromise demanded by the preservation conscious-ness relating to the Canongate at that time.

The internal configuration of the building does little to suggest that the elevational treatments applied to the Canongate façades were anything more than that.

The 'tower' element of the Canongate façade, where the stairwell might be expected to be located, is in fact floored out and consists of a single room at each level (Figure 1.23), the actual stairwell taking up the whole of the remaining accommodation fronting onto Canongate, where a more substantial hallway might be expected (Figures 1.28 and 1.29).

The main accommodation of the building is all located within the modern brick rear section (Figures 1.27 and 1.31).

In terms of genuine importance, the brick rear of the building has some relatively well-considered art deco detailing, but essentially takes on the appearance of being the lesser part. The random rubble-clad front part of the building is materially responsive to the character of the Canongate. However, its set-back entrance and pretension to some greater use presently fail to activate the street frontage, creating an incongruous open space at this location (Figure 1.23).

It should be considered that, if the present Canongate façade fronted a building with an active public use, the set back on the Canongate would provide a much more relevant and vibrant space.

In terms of its individual importance within the Old Town, neither the Old Town Conservation Area character appraisal nor the World Heritage Site management plan makes specific reference to it. In this respect, it is not specifically acknowledged to be part of the essential character of either the Conservation Area or the World Heritage Site.

In this case the relative importance of the building was considered to be a mitigating factor rather than a principal justification for its partial demolition.

Condition

The condition of the building was a principal factor in justifying the demolition of the rear of the building. In this respect, Arups were commissioned to produce a substantial structural report, which was, in turn, appended to the Heritage Statement. The following 'umbrella' section was included in the Heritage Statement itself:

Condition

Arup Scotland undertook a visual inspection of the condition of the Sailor's Ark in October 2005. In this respect they reported a number of significant problems, including:

- Roof gutters are in a poor state of repair.
- Movement of brickwork at chimneys and parapets.
- Defective roof covering.
- Missing coping stones.
- Deterioration of masonry pointing.
- Defective structural detailing of window openings within brickwork.
- Potential failure of brick external leaf.

Regarding the brick external leaf, the Structural Report states that the external leaf of the brick wall is in poor condition and is suffering from corrosion of embedded steelwork. The worst affected areas are presently at roof level on the west elevation, which is exposed to the prevailing winds. However, it is likely that the remaining elevations are affected by similar problems and that continuing corrosion to the exposed steelwork and the cavity wall ties will eventually lead to the instability of the outer leaf of brickwork and potential collapse of sections of the wall.

In terms of Clause 2.10 of the Memorandum of Guidance, while many of the defects identified are examples of poor maintenance over a number of years, the failure of the external brickwork at the rear part of the building must be considered to be of a serious structural nature.

Alternative use

The future viability of the building in realistic alternative use was a further principal justification:

Alternative Use

The basement level of the Old Sailor's Ark, accessed from New Street, remains in use as a feeding centre for homeless people. The upper level accommodation has lain empty for a number of years.

Within its present context it is conceivable that the Old Sailor's Ark can be adapted to some alternative use – possibly low quality office use. However, given the structural problems with the external brick cladding at the part of the building housing its main accommodation, its continued viability is affected by the significant costs that will arise from rectifying this problem. These will be further affected by the costs associated with reconfiguration and addressing the considerable mainten-ance issues. In this regard a disproportionate level of investment would be required to ensure a sustainable future for the building in its present form.

A development appraisal demonstrating the disproportionate level of investment that would be required was produced and submitted separately to the planning authority as additional supporting information.

Thereafter, the benefits to be derived from the development were discussed in terms of the supplementary planning guidance included in the adopted Caltongate master plan and the redevelopment of the Old Sailor's Ark within this context:

Caltongate master plan

Regarding Listed Buildings the Caltongate master plan notes:

The Council will seek to retain and re-use listed buildings. How-ever, it is also recognised that there may be circumstances where a case can be made that outweighs the individual historic and architectural value of the buildings, such as the benefits of a regeneration scheme, the planning benefits gained and the quality of the replacement buildings.

Where it is proposed to alter an existing listed building, the determining factor will be the impact of the work on the character of the building as a building of special architectural or historic interest.

Specifically in relation to the Old Sailor's Ark, the master plan states:

The main architectural or historic interest is in the front stone section and this should be retained largely unaltered including the existing doorpiece.

The demolition of the rear portion could be considered favourably but the quality of the replacement building and its integration with the front section will be a key factor in this determination.

Throughout the master plan document, the front portion of the Sailor's Ark is shown as an integral part of the five-star hotel, providing the principal reception entrance from the Canongate.

Caltongate Development Project

The proposals for the Old Sailor's Ark are integral to the wider proposals presented in detail in the drawings and documents supporting the detailed Planning, Listed Building and Conservation Area Consent submissions to the City of Edinburgh Council. In this regard they are included within Planning Application PA5 and Listed Building Consent Application LBC1.

The conceptual design for PA5, the Hotel and Conference Centre, has been undertaken by RWHL, an internationally renowned Architect's Practice specialising in hotel design of the highest quality. The contextual design has been undertaken by Page & Park, a leading Scottish design practice, who specialise in careful, analytical architectural responses to historically sensitive urban sites.

The site of the Old Sailor's Ark is required to be developed to form part of the five-star Hotel and Conference Centre, essential to the implementation of the master plan.

The configuration and type of accommodation provided by the existing building is not convertible to such a use. Consequently within the context of the master plan the substantial integration of the Old Sailor's Ark is not feasible.

However, it is recognised that the Canongate façade of the building is an existing element in terms of the character and appearance of the Old Town at this location and that its present configuration is well suited to providing an entrance of some character. In this regard it is proposed to retain the Canongate façade (continuing into New Street) as the important Canongate entrance to the new five star Hotel.

The Ark's existing community function will be relocated in new accommodation to be created at Calton Road North under the wider Caltongate Development Project.

In line with all the individual cases for Listed Builidng/Conservation Area consent, the case was summarized in a concluding section:

Conclusion

In terms of Paragraph 2.10 of the Memorandum of Guidance the Old Sailor's Ark is a relatively incongruous building of local importance, whose most significant feature is its overstated Canongate façade. As an individual building it is not specifically acknowledged to be part of the essential character of either the Conservation Area or the World Heritage Site.

The rear portion of the existing building is structurally unsound and a disproportionate level of investment would be required to repair and return it to viable use.

The site on which the Old Sailor's Ark presently stands is essential to the implementation of the wider Caltongate master plan and is of considerable importance in terms of the benefits that will be derived therefrom. The Sailor's Ark cannot feasibly accommodate the five star Hotel function required at this location.

Paragraph 2.11 of the Memorandum of Guidance recognises that the advantages foreseen for new development need to be carefully weighed against the value to the community of preserving and possibly enhancing the existing environment.

The site's proposed new use and the significant new building accommodating that use, coupled with the recycled use of the retained façade as a principal entrance, will create a vitality and vibrancy necessary to reactivate this part of the Canongate, positively enhancing both the existing environment and the setting of other adjacent listed buildings.

The partial loss of the Old Sailor's Ark, as a Category C(S) Listed Building, will be regrettable. However, this will be mitigated by the retention of its Canongate façade in a use genuinely reflective of its original design. This will effectively preserve the appearance of the existing Canongate at this location whilst significantly enhancing its character.

On balance, it is considered that the substantial demolition of the building will be considerably outweighed by the city-wide benefits that will be gained by the implementation of the Caltongate master plan and the quality of the replacement hotel building, which will retain the Canongate façade, and will positively enhance both the Old Town and the setting of other listed buildings in the area.

The setting of Listed Buildings

Again, I have included below, in full with comments, the section of the Heritage Statement dealing with the setting of Listed Buildings:

Setting of Listed Buildings

Introduction

The impact of the Caltongate Development Project on the setting of listed buildings located within its vicinity is considered in this section. In this respect importance is apportioned to the listed building or structure remaining the focus of its essential setting.

There will be an impact upon the setting of the following Listed Buildings located within or within the vicinity of the development site:

Royal High School, Regent Road	Category A Listed
St Andrew's House, Regent Road	Category A Listed
Governor's House (formerly of Calton Jail)	Category A Listed
Regent Road retaining wall	Category B Listed
Monuments on Calton Hill	Category A Listed
Calton Old Burying Ground and Monuments	Category A Listed
Canongate Parish Church	Category A Listed
Canongate Parish Church Churchyard	Category B Listed
167–169 Canongate (Tollbooth Tavern)	Category A Listed
183–187 Canongate (Bible Land)	Category B Listed
189 – 191 Canongate (Flats 2, 4 and 6)	Category B Listed
191 Canongate (Flats 1, 3 and 5)	Category B Listed
195–197 Canongate (Shoemaker's Land)	Category B Listed
249–263 Canongate and 43 New Street (Morocco Land)	Category B Listed
265–267 Canongate (Morocco Land)	Category B Listed
271 Canongate (former Canongate United Presbyterian Church)	Category C(S) Listed
174 Canongate (Moray House)	Category A Listed
176–184 Canongate	Category C(S) Listed
194–198 Canongate (Old Playhouse Close)	Category B Listed
3–37 Jeffrey Street	Category B Listed
4–18 Jeffrey Street and 3–9 Cranston Street	Category B Listed
Jeffrey Street, wall, vaults, railings and pier	Category C(S) Listed

It is useful to consider these buildings under the following broad headings:

- Listed Buildings and Monuments on Calton Hill/Regent Road;
- Listed Buildings in the Canongate; and
- Listed Buildings in Jeffrey Street/Cranston Street.

Design of the development proposals

In assessing the impact of the development proposals on the setting of adjacent listed buildings it is important to consider that the design of these proposals is of a very high quality, guided by detailed contextual analysis and the principles set out in the Caltongate master plan, which are specifically intended to minimise the impact of development upon the existing built environment. It has also been the subject of extensive consultation.

Listed Buildings and monuments on Calton Hill/Regent Road

The significant listed (and unlisted) buildings and structures on Calton Hill/Regent Road whose settings will be affected are:

- Royal High School, Regent Road;
- St Andrew's House, Regent Road;
- Governor's House (formerly of Calton Jail);
- Monuments on Calton Hill;
- Regent Road retaining wall.

Views towards Calton Hill/Regent Road

In relation to the Caltongate Development Project the present essential setting of the listed buildings and monuments on Calton Hill and Regent Road is their position overlooking Waverley Valley from atop the rocky escarpment and scree rising steeply above Calton Road. Due to this elevated position they will remain the focus of their immediate setting in views towards Calton Hill.

The principal existing views towards Calton Hill and Regent Road from across and within the Valley are generally provided by accident rather than by specific intent. From the Canongate these are from the Canongate Parish Church and Churchyard and down Tolbooth Wynd and New Street (Figures 1.25 and 1.33). There are also views across the semi-derelict former Bus Garage site from Gladstone Court.

Moving west the principal views are from the junction of the Canongate, St Mary's Street, and Jeffrey Street, and from Cranston Street. Travelling down Jeffrey Street views to the north east open up from the Jeffrey Street railings, where the building line on the east side of the street was discontinued (Figure 1.34). There are panoramic views towards Calton Hill and Regent Road from the west part of East Market Street, although these, and views from Cranston Street, have been affected by the new Council Headquarters building (Figure 1.6).

The proposed development incorporates a number of specifically designed new framed views towards Calton Hill. From the Canongate, Nelson's Monument will be framed by the views from the new Canongate connection and travelling down the new pedestrian street. The link passage across New Street will screen the utilitarian railway bridge at the foot of the street in the framed view towards St Andrew's House (Figure 1.32).

The realignment of Cranston Street will create a directed view towards Governor's House from the Canongate, Jeffrey Street, St Mary's Street junction.

The viewing gallery at the proposed new landmark building on East Market Street will create panoramic views to the west, south and east that will compensate for the loss of passive eastward views resulting from the resolution of the East Market Street gap site.

Views from Calton Hill/Regent Road

Existing views from the listed features on Calton Hill/Regent Road take in the present semi-derelict, redundant and utilitarian nature of the Waverley

Valley at this location [Figure 1.1]. The principal existing features on the other side of the valley are the Canongate ridge, although this is almost obscured locally by the Old Sailor's Ark; and the rhythmic Jeffrey Street Vaults as they return and increase in height up the Valley, and the not unexceptional designed gable end of 4–18 Jeffrey Street and 3–9 Cranston Street, both fully exposed by the unresolved gap site at East Market Street (Figure 1.7).

The development proposals for the sites in the immediate foreground of the escarpment will individually regenerate the southern bank of the Waverley Valley from Calton Road to the back of the Canongate (Figure 1.2). In each instance the heights of the buildings are guided by the Caltongate master plan and the pre-eminence of the Canongate ridge in views across the valley will be maintained. The east end of East Market Street, which is already partially screened by the new Council headquarters building will be almost completely obscured in views from Calton Hill.

The creation of the new landmark building that is intended to resolve the existing East Market Street gap site and to provide a properly

1.33
**Former Bus Garage,
New Street (courtesy
of Allan Murray
Architects)**

1.34
View toward Calton Hill from Jeffrey Street (courtesy of Allan Murray Architects)

defined southern edge to the Old Town at this location will provide a new defining focal point in views towards East Market Street and Jeffrey Street, from Calton Hill and Regent Road.

Listed Buildings and monuments on Calton Hill/Regent Road: conclusions

The implementation of the Caltongate Development Project will significantly enhance the setting of the Listed Buildings and Monuments on Calton Hill and Regent Road, by the carefully controlled regenerative nature of the project.

Listed Buildings in the Canongate

The significant Listed (and unlisted) Buildings in the Canongate whose settings will be affected are:

- Canongate Parish Church;
- Canongate Parish Church, Churchyard;
- 183–187 Canongate (Bible Land);
- 189–191 Canongate (Flats 2, 4 and 6);

- 191 Canongate (Flats 1, 3 and 5);
- 195–197 Canongate (Shoemaker's Land);
- 249–263 Canongate and 43 New Street (Morocco Land);
- 265–267 Canongate (Morocco Land);
- 194–198 Canongate (Old Playhouse Close);
- 231 Canongate (Old Sailor's Ark);
- 174 Canongate (Moray House)
- 176–184 Canongate;
- 271 Canongate (former Canongate United Presbyterian Church);
- 2 Cranston Street (former Canongate Christian Institute).

Principal settings

The principal setting of all of the Canongate tenements is the Canongate and their interrelationship with it. In this respect the only direct impacts on the Canongate, under the development proposals, will be the new connection from the new square and 'Parliament Way', and the remodelling of the retained façades of 227–229 and the Old Sailor's Ark, to create new shopfronts and the Canongate entrance to the proposed five-star hotel. Both of which have been specifically designed to minimise the impact on the appearance of the Canongate itself (Figures 1.4, 1.16, 1.21 and 1.22).

These alterations are such that in views towards the Canongate façades of Nos. 176–184, 183–187, 189–191, 191, 194–198, 195–197, 249–263 and 265–267, from within the Canongate, each building will remain the focus of its essential setting.

In views out from each of these buildings only 174, 176–184 and 194–198 on the south side of the street will have anything more than an oblique view of the changes. It may be considered that the creation of the new street connection immediately across the Canongate from Nos. 176–184 will enhance the setting and indeed the use of its pended access to St John's Street (new views towards the pend will be created).

Secondary settings

The existing secondary setting to the rear of Nos. 167–169, 183–187, 189–191, 191, 195–197, 221–223, 227–229 and 231 Canongate is a semi private area (Gladstone Land) consisting of a car park, accessed from the Canongate, on its eastern part, and fenced off drying greens to the area adjacent the rear part of the Old Sailor's Ark (Figure 1.27). Without the containment of an opposite façade, the rear elevations of these tenements, take on an austere overbearing appearance. The concrete framed landings at the rear elevation of Nos. 227–229 Canongate are distinctly utilitarian.

There are existing views from Nos. 183–187, 189–191, 191 and 195–197 towards Calton Hill across the site of the now demolished former bus depot.

The development proposals will properly establish Gladstone Court as a relevant and intimate courtyard setting. Secondary wynds and stairs will provide new northward permeability from the Gladstone Court towards Old Tolbooth Wynd and Calton Road in a manner reflecting the herring bone pattern of expansion on the High Street.

The existing secondary setting to the rear of Nos. 249–263 and 265–267 and 271 Canongate (former Canongate United Presbyterian Church) and 2 Cranston Street (former Canongate Christian Institute) is contained by the retaining wall at the back of Canongate Venture and the disused Car Depot on East Market Street. The new Council headquarters building impinges to some extent upon views from the upper storeys of the tenements across the valley.

The proposals for the new five star hotel and conference centre, and mixed use building adjacent (development proposals PA 5 and PA 6) will maintain the existing retaining boundary wall, consequently the immediate essentially courtyard setting to the rear of the Canongate tenements will be preserved. Beyond the retaining wall, the proposed hotel and mixed use accommodation will enclose views northward. In both instances these developments will provide designed façades and planted semi private courtyards, accessed by pends and stairs from New Street, Cranston Street and East Market Street, orientated towards the rear of the existing Canongate buildings. Thus providing a relevant new courtyard setting beyond the retaining wall.

2 Cranston Street (former Canongate Christian Institute)

The principal setting of 2 Cranston Street (former Canongate Christian Institute) is the low-walled garden ground of 271 Canongate (former Canongate United Presbyterian Church) at the corner of Cranston Street and the Canongate, and the tenements on the west side of Cranston Street. The utilitarian Car Depot to its north and the unresolved nature of the foot of Cranston Street are considered to be incongruous.

The development proposals will have a negligible effect on the principal setting of 2 Cranston Street. Development proposals PA 6 and PA 7 will knit the disparate elements at the foot of Cranston Street into a new urban fabric that will provide new urban definition to this area. 2 Cranston Street will become an important element in this setting.

Canongate Parish Church and Churchyard

The essential setting of Canongate Parish Church centres on its relationship with the Canongate, significantly more so than any existing relationship with Calton Road. The principal backdrop to the Church looking northwards from the Canongate is the Royal High School, Regent Road Wall and Calton Hill. In this regard it can be seen that existing new developments on Calton Road, which are of a similar (or in the case of the

Barratt development considerably greater) scale to that proposed, will only have a limited affect on views from the Canongate.

The presence of the existing new developments becomes clearer in views from the rear of the Church northwards. However, even here, the presence of the High School and Calton Hill remains the dominant setting. The low lying nature of Calton Road and the limited height of the proposed new residential blocks will ensure that this will continue on completion of the proposed development.

Whilst the existing building at 20 Calton Road is not as high as the proposed new residential building and the roof pitches away from the Churchyard, its semi derelict and incongruous appearance creates a poor setting immediately adjacent the north western boundary of the Churchyard (Figure 1.17). The proposed new residential building(s) will relate to other ongoing residential development along Calton Road.

Calton Road lies at a significantly lower level than the Church and Churchyard and views from here towards both are largely obscured by the existing retaining wall. A retaining boundary wall partly obscures views towards the church from Tolbooth Wynd. However, the general perception of open space associated with the Churchyard will be undiminished by the new building.

It should be considered that whilst a secondary part of the existing setting of the Canongate Churchyard and Church will be altered by the redevelopment of the redundant sites on either side of Calton Road, attention to both will be no more distracted than it is at present. Indeed the improved general appearance of Calton Road at this location may be considered to improve the secondary setting of both (Figures 1.5 and 1.19).

Listed buildings in the Canongate: conclusions

The implementation of the Caltongate Development Project will enhance the essential settings of the Listed Buildings in and around the Canongate.

The secondary settings of these buildings, which are presently generally orientated towards semi-derelict sites or utilitarian buildings, will be enhanced by the carefully controlled regenerative nature of the project.

Listed Buildings in Jeffrey Street/Cranston Street

The significant Listed (and unlisted) Buildings in the vicinity of Jeffrey Street/Cranston Street whose settings will be affected are:

- 3–37 Jeffrey Street;
- 4–18 Jeffrey Street and 3–9 Cranston Street; and
- Jeffrey Street, wall, vaults, railings and pier – PA 7, PA 1–7.

3–37 Jeffrey Street

The existing principal setting of 3–37 Jeffrey Street is the Canongate, Jeffrey Street, St Mary's Street junction, the double sided upper part of Jeffrey Street, the shopfronts at street level, and the open views towards and from Calton Hill (Figure 1.34).

The proposed PA 7 development, the new defining landmark building, will restrict views across the Waverley Valley to and from the east and from street level. Views northwards will be restricted by the two-storey portion of the proposed development (although it should be noted that it is views towards and from the lower part of the escarpment and Waverley Station goods yards).

The immediate setting of the tenements will be improved by the continuation of an active street front on the east side of Jeffrey Street (Figures 1.8 and 1.34). The proposed new stairs will provide framed viewpoints in approaches from East Market Street and Cranston Street.

Cranston Street façade of 3–9 Cranston Street

The immediate urban setting of the Cranston Street façade of 3–9 Cranston Street will be improved by the redevelopment of the Car Depot site and the gap site on East Market Street (proposed PA 6 and PA 7 developments). However, in long views towards and from this façade, the PA6 proposal will obstruct views.

Jeffrey Street façade of 4–18 Jeffrey Street

The main part of the Jeffrey Street façade of 4–18 Jeffrey Street will be largely unaffected by the development proposals, although the proposed PA 7 development will clearly figure in oblique views to and from the building.

The principal impact upon the existing setting of 4–18 Jeffrey Street and 3–9 Cranston Street

The principal impact upon the existing setting of 4–18 Jeffrey Street and 3–9 Cranston Street will be at the northern, gable end of the building. The present long views towards this part of the tenement will be obstructed by the proposed PA 7 and PA 6 developments. However, whilst the tenement is acknowledged to have a designed terminating gable end, it should be considered that this was only devised as an afterthought when it was decided to discontinue the street and is not of an urban quality that merits its existing widely exposed location (Figure 1.7).

In terms of urban setting, it is considered that the proposed PA 7 development will provide a more relevant close setting to the designed gable wall that will emphasize the gable corner turrets, which in turn will become important elements within a number of immediately adjacent redefined urban spaces (the stairs from Cranston Street, views up and down Jeffrey Street). In this regard the creation of a more defined southern edge to the Old Town at this location is considered to justify the redefinition of the existing building's setting.

Jeffrey Street, wall, vaults, railings and pier

The existing immediate essential setting of Jeffrey Street, wall, vaults, railings and pier is confined to East Market Street and the gap site at the junction with Cranston Street, although the structure clearly figures in the long views from Calton Hill discussed above (Figures 1.1, 1.6 and 1.7).

The proposed public realm improvements will significantly improve both the setting of the exposed redeveloped Vaults (Vaults 1–18).

Whilst the proposed PA 7 development will change the setting of Vaults 19–24, the transparency of the building at street level is intended to permit views towards the curving wall. Notwithstanding that the PA 7 proposal is intended to resolve the presently unsatisfactory urban appearance at this location, the curved nature of Jeffrey Street will remain a feature of views from North Bridge and Calton Hill (Figure 1.2).

Listed Buildings in Jeffrey Street/Cranston Street: conclusions

The creation of the new landmark building, intended to resolve the existing East Market Street gap site and to provide a properly defined southern edge to the Old Town at this location, will have a considerable impact on the existing setting of the listed buildings on Jeffrey Street and the Jeffrey Street Arches. However, it requires to be acknowledged that the existing setting for the listed buildings is poorly defined in wider urban terms, and not entirely relevant to the limited urban qualities of the buildings themselves (continuous tenemental blocks and an essentially utilitarian supporting structure for Jeffrey Street).

In this respect it is considered that the redefined urban environment is relevant, and indeed will enhance the immediate setting of these buildings.

Conclusions

In assessing the impact of the development proposals on the setting of adjacent listed buildings it is important to consider that the design of these proposals is of a very high quality, guided by detailed contextual analysis and the principles set out in the Caltongate master plan, which are specifically intended to minimise the impact of development upon the existing built environment. It has also been the subject of extensive consultation.

The minimisation of local impacts on the Canongate will ensure that each listed building on the Canongate will remain the focus of its essential setting. Indeed relevant new framed views and the remodelling of the street frontages of 227–231 may be considered to enhance the setting of those immediately adjacent.

The redefinition of the immediate settings of the buildings at Jeffrey Street is relevant and indeed will enhance the immediate setting of these buildings.

The creation of the new landmark building that is intended to resolve the existing East Market Street gap site will enhance the southern edge of the Old Town at this location.

The preservation or enhancement of the Old Town Conservation Area

The case regarding the preservation or enhancement of the Old Town Conservation Area is included below. It deliberately used specific characteristics and key elements incorporated within the character appraisal published by the City of Edinburgh Council, and specific omissions in this regard, to demonstrate the actual impact that the proposals would have:

Impact on Old Town Conservation Area: essential characteristics

Introduction

Within this Section, the impact of the Caltongate Development Project on the special architectural and visual qualities that gave rise to the designation of the Old Town Conservation Area is considered.

NPPG 18 states that, in considering applications for planning permission affecting conservation areas, proposals should be assessed in terms of their impact upon the character or appearance of the whole conservation area and that, where it can be demonstrated that parts of individual areas are of a different character, proposals can be assessed in terms of the character of these individual areas.

Three distinct areas within the Old Town Conservation Area will be affected by the development proposals:

- The eastern part of the Waverley Valley.
- The top of the Canongate.
- East Market Street and Jeffrey Street.

Design of the development proposals

In assessing the impact of the development proposals on the special architectural and visual qualities that gave rise to the designation of the Old Town Conservation Area it is important to consider that the design of these proposals has been guided by the principles set out in the Caltongate master plan, which are specifically intended to minimise the impact of development upon the existing built environment, and have been the subject of extensive consultation.

The eastern part of the Waverley Valley

The character and appearance of the part of the Old Town Conservation Area at this location are significantly different to that described within the formal Character Appraisal for the Old Town Conservation Area. In this respect it is acknowledged to be detrimental to that of the wider Conservation Area and the World Heritage Site (Figure 1.1).

The top of the Canongate

Within the Canongate, which genuinely does contribute to the special qualities of the wider area, the actual character and appearance of the thoroughfare, from New Street to Moray House, the area directly affected by the Development, is different to that described for the rest of the Canongate and the wider Conservation Area (Figures 1.16 and 1.22).

East Market Street and Jeffrey Street

Again, at East Market Street and Jeffrey Street, the existing character and appearance does not reflect the special architectural and visual qualities described in the Character Appraisal (Figures 1.6, 1.7 and 1.34). Whilst clearly the existing urban configuration forms part of the existing views across the Valley, it is not of a genuine urban quality relevant to the southern edge of the Old Town.

Impact on the essential character of the Conservation Area

The Memorandum of Guidance and Passed to the Future both acknowledge that it is a Conservation Area's special architectural and visual qualities that must be given primacy in the consideration of proposed new development.

In this regard, Passed to the Future (Historic Scotland 2002) acknowledges that the historic environment is not static and that it has a dynamic and positive contribution to make to society, that it has been continually adapted to meet changing needs over a very long period of time, and that underlying concepts of what is important develop and change. It accepts that new environments are created and become historic in time and states that the challenge in managing the historic environment sustainably, and in a way which contributes to the vitality of modern life, is to identify its key characteristics and to establish the parameters within which change can continue so that it enhances rather than diminishes historic character.

A broad assessment of the impact of the overall Caltongate Development Project upon relevant essential qualities of the Old Town Conservation Area, as set out in the Character Appraisal, is summarised in the following table. A similar summary is provided for the impact of the individual development proposals within Table 7.12 of the Cultural Heritage Chapter of the Environmental Statement:

Relevant Essential Qualities set out in the Conservation Area Character Appraisal	Caltongate development project
Spatial structure	
The spatial structure of the Old Town is a microcosm of urban development, reflecting the multiple layering of built heritage and responding to the drama of the site's topography and setting . . .	The development proposals reflect a further layer of built heritage, designed to the highest contemporary standards, reflecting the evolving requirements of the city and responding to the site's topography and setting.
The contrast in density and built form between the original walled city and relative openness of Canongate . . .	The creation of the new square is representative of the greater openness of the Canongate Burgh (Figure 1.3). However, the existing site has been built on, and evolving in a utilitarian manner, for over 200 years.
The survival of the original medieval street pattern overlaid with late 19th century improvements in organic forms responding to the contours . . .	There is nothing remaining of the original medieval street pattern (except perhaps locally at the Canongate). Where the 19th century overlay is impacted upon, at Jeffrey Street, the development proposals intend to address the unresolved gap that resulted from the decision not to complete the east side of the street. The development proposals introduce a new hierarchy of streets and wynds that reflect historic development from the Royal Mile into the Waverley Valley. Importantly, the new connection into the Canongate is located on the site of 'Big Jack's Close'.
Dramatic gateways created over the Waverley Valley . . .	A primary objective of the overall development proposal is to provide a necessary contemporary route between the Waverley and emerging Holyrood utilising an area that is incongruous with the character and appearance of the wider Conservation Area. New routes from and to Regent Road and Calton Hill will be created.
Townscape	
The clear definition and drama of much of the northern, western and south–eastern edge of the area, particularly the visibility of the Castle and the Old Town ridge from all over Edinburgh . . .	The views across the Waverley Valley from Calton Hill, at this specific location, will be significantly improved by the replacement of the present semi-derelict appearance of the Waverley Valley at this specific location. The pre-eminent views of the Canongate Ridge will be maintained. The height of the new buildings is guided by Principle 6 of the Caltongate master plan.
A wide range of institutional buildings from different eras set against a backdrop of tenements contributing to an appearance of density, a 'close-knit' character and cohesive groupings associated with a medieval town . . .	The present appearance of the development area within is one of utilitarian openness. The development proposals will create a regulated density and a number of significant new contemporary buildings set against the tenements along the Old Town ridge. In this regard the precedent for contemporary buildings within the Waverley Valley has already been set by the Council Headquarters Building.

continued . . .

. . . continued

Relevant Essential Qualities set out in the Conservation Area Character Appraisal	Caltongate development project
Townscape . . . continued	
The variety and irregularity of medieval buildings contrast with imposed styling of later 'improvement act' architecture . . .	The development area does not accord with this description. The wider existing contrast between medieval buildings and 'improvement act' architecture will be undiminished by the development proposals.
Pitched roof forms give an interest by stepped and angled roofscapes articulated by narrow dormers, crowstepped gables, pediments, towers, spires, skews, chimneyheads, and so on.	The development area (with the exception of the Canongate Venture and the tenements on the Canongate) does not accord with this description. The detailed design of the new buildings will be guided by the Caltongate master plan.
The hard-edged nature of the main streets and spaces within the area formed by the continuous frontages of tall buildings built directly up to the back of pavements . . .	While the existing utilitarian buildings in the development area can be seen to come to the back of the pavement (with the exception of the Canongate Venture), they fail to provide genuine frontages that properly interact with the street. The development proposals will create new back of pavement frontages that will genuinely reflect the hard-edged nature of the main streets within the Old Town.
The clarity of the streetscape due to the limited palette of natural stone materials . . .	The existing development area, generally, does not accord with this description. The Canongate Venture is constructed of Red Sandstone, the existing garage and rear of the Ark are of red brick. The developments propose the predominant use of traditional materials in accordance with Principle 11 of the Caltongate master plan, other relevant existing design guidance and precedent, which will complement the existing materials. The existing Canongate frontages will largely be retained.
The simple layout of streets, consisting of a carriageway flanked by pavements running directly from kerb line to building frontage . . .	The development proposals will reflect this characteristic where it does not presently exist and will retain it on the Canongate and elsewhere.
The high level of pedestrian permeability throughout the Old Town.	There is specifically a poor level of 'permeability' throughout the Old Town at the location of the development area. A specific intention of the development is to address this deficiency.
Architectural character	
The architectural coherence and authenticity of setting and historic context.	There is virtually no architectural coherence, authenticity of setting and historic context across the existing development area. The utilitarian redevelopment of the area over very many years creates a distinct incoherence. The development proposals will provide a coherent new

continued . . .

. . . continued

Relevant Essential Qualities set out in the Conservation Area Character Appraisal	Caltongate development project
Architectural character . . . continued	

	identity for the area that makes genuine reference to its historical context. The existing Canongate frontage at this location dates from the 1930s and arguably had a detrimental impact upon its wider character and appearance.
The landmark buildings which make a contribution to the City's historic skyline.	There are no genuine landmark buildings within the existing development area that genuinely contribute to the City's skyline, although the pre-eminence of the Canongate ridge is acknowledged. While the development proposals will result in a high quality of modern architecture across the area, these are not intended to impact upon the historic skyline.
The survival of an outstanding collection of archaeological remains, medieval buildings and 17th-century town houses.	The development proposals will specify archaeological investigations in accordance with the Regional Archaeologist's requirements. The proposal will not physically impact upon any medieval buildings or 17th- century town houses.
The outstanding collection of statutes, monuments, historic graveyards and national memorials.	There are no statues, monuments, historic graveyards or national memorials within the existing development area. The graveyard at the Canongate Kirk is physically unaffected by the proposals.
The consistent and harmonious height and mass of buildings: usually four or five storeys high of street frontages.	The existing height and mass of buildings in the development area do not accord with this description. The development proposals will create a contemporary 'tenemental' scale and massing that are consistent and relevant within the context of the tenements along the Canongate. The Canongate façades will remain largely as at present.
The proportion and rhythm of building frontages, determined by ownership patterns of both the original mediaeval 'Burgess' plots and later tenement layouts.	The development area does not accord with this description. The proportion and rhythm of the new buildings will make reference to tenemental plot sizes and frontages. The Canongate façades will remain largely as at present.
The quality, robustness and durability of the materials of construction.	The development proposals will provide buildings of the highest contemporary quality. The developments propose the predominant use of traditional materials in accordance with Principle 11 of the Caltongate master plan, other relevant existing design guidance and precedent.
The importance of stone as a construction material for both buildings and the public realm.	
The use of high quality natural materials and workmanship for paving and street finishes.	

continued . . .

. . . continued

Relevant Essential Qualities set out in the Conservation Area Character Appraisal	Caltongate development project
Architectural character . . . continued	
The limited pallet of building materials, mainly stone and slate, provide a unity of character.	The unifying nature of natural stone is an acknowledged element of the developments. This is also reflected in proposals for the public realm.
The importance of the archaeological record.	The development proposals will specify archaeological investigations in accordance with the Regional Archaeologist's requirements.
Natural heritage	
A landscape and topography formed by vigorous geological activity.	The essential underlying landscape and topography will be unaffected by the development proposals.
The regular pattern of open green spaces shaped by topography and historic development.	The development area does not accord with this description.
The quality of long-distance views, both open and framed in, out and through the spaces, and the views from different levels and idiosyncratic angles.	The quality of existing long views across the Waverley Valley is significantly affected by the utilitarian and semi-derelict nature of the development area. The development proposals will specifically create new framed views and viewpoints between the Old and New Town and within the development area. There will be a loss of some of the accidental views created when it was decided not to complete the east side of Jeffrey Street.
Management regimes, from naturalistic to high maintenance, which correspond appropriately to the location and use of open spaces.	The existing development site is not governed by any specific management regime. The overall development proposal includes the provision of management regimes dealing with the maintenance of both private and public realm spaces.
Landscape design styles which reflect the shapes and forms of the surrounding architectural environment.	The existing development area does not accord with this description. The development proposals will establish designed landscapes following existing design policies and guidance where appropriate.
Areas with high bio-diversity significance with unusual species.	The existing development area does not accord with this description.
A wealth of hidden, enclosed spaces characterised by their individuality. These are mainly accessible to the pedestrian only through curved arches, gates and narrow closes.	There are no existing hidden or enclosed spaces of any quality that will be impacted upon by the development proposals (the land to the rear of the Canongate tenements generally provides enclosed spaces of poor quality). The development proposals will create many such spaces.

continued . . .

. . . continued

Relevant Essential Qualities set out in the Conservation Area Character Appraisal	Caltongate development project
Natural heritage . . . continued	
The use of high-quality paving material and sculptural elements within the spaces.	While there are areas of high-quality paving materials within the Canongate and the western end of Market Street, there are no other areas of high-quality paving or sculptural elements within the existing development area. The specification of a new high-quality public realm will be guided by Principle 11 of the Caltongate master plan and other existing design policy and precedent.
The presence of a few selective individual or groups of forest scale and small trees providing a setting for buildings and creating focal points.	The existing development area does not accord with this description. The overall proposal generally calls for high-quality hard landscaping. Although it is proposed to line the new residential street and part of East Market Street with trees and to introduce trees within the new square.
High-quality boundary elements including stone walls frequently of a high and sinuous form. The use of appropriate and often individualistically designed iron railings and gates, often of a curved or arched form.	The Jeffrey Street wall and railings and those at the Canongate Venture are Category C(S) Listed and may be considered to correspond to this description. Whilst probably the most characterful features within the existing development area they are not the principal examples of these types of elements within the wider Conservation Area. It should also be considered that the boundary wall to the Canongate Venture is the principle element sterilising the existing street frontage.
Activities and uses	
The numerous important institutional and public service uses that contribute to its character and the nation's character.	The existing development area provides no important institutional and public service uses of this nature (although the new Council Headquarters building, adjacent, may be considered to be a contemporary example). The development proposal will improve the environment and connections across the Canongate/Holyrood area which will actively sustain and improve these existing important uses and encourage further use by civic and institutional functions.
The vitality and variety of different uses which contribute to the character of the Conservation Area.	There is limited vitality within the existing development area. A principal intention of the development proposals is to establish a new vitality and variety of uses within the area that will sustain the new district and create interaction with the wider Conservation Area.
The strong and continuing presence of a residential community.	Existing residential use within the development area is restricted to the tenements (221–229) on the Canongate. However, the wider Canongate and Jeffrey Street have strong existing communities. The development will improve the vitality and connections within these areas, encouraging continuing residential usage.

continued . . .

. . . continued

Relevant Essential Qualities set out in the Conservation Area Character Appraisal	Caltongate development project
Activities and uses . . . continued	
Increasing residential development is ensuring a living town centre.	The proposals (PA 1 and PA 4) will create substantial new residential locations in the hinterland of the Canongate and will ensure a strong continuing residential presence in this part of the Old Town.
Mixed uses at ground floor level are important in securing active streets and 'Street life'.	The existing development area is blighted by long stretches of 'sterile' street frontage. A specific aim of the development proposals is to create active street frontages that interrelate with the adjacent streets as a driver to create vitality in the area. The development proposals will address the austere nature of the existing frontage at 221–231 Canongate, remodelling the existing elevations to provide the new five star hotel entrance onto the Canongate, and shop units encouraging pedestrians into the Canongate from High Street.

New Development

NPPG 18 states that, if a proposed development would have negative and positive impacts, these would require to be weighed against each other and the proposals considered as a whole.

The Memorandum of Guidance states that new development that is well designed, respects the character of the area and contributes to its enhancement should be welcome. It also acknowledges that control rather than prevention can allow an area to remain alive and prosperous but at the same time ensure that new development accords with the special architectural and visual qualities of the Conservation Area.

The design of the development proposals is of a high contextual quality and has been guided by the principles set out in the Caltongate master plan.

The limited physical loss of the existing building fabric within the parts of the Old Town Conservation Area relating to the Development, whose character and appearance is identifiably different from the whole, will be a localised impact. It can be seen that the benefits that the development proposals will bring to the character and appearance of the local and wider Conservation Area, are positive city-wide benefits that must be seen to outweigh these limited losses.

Conclusion

Whilst it is acknowledged that the Caltongate Development Proposal will have a localised physical impact upon the Old Town Conservation Area, it can be seen that any negative impact upon its recognised essential characteristics is marginal when considered in terms of the social, economic and cultural benefits that will be derived and the contextual quality of the design. Rather, any perceivable impacts upon what are the Old Town's essential qualities have been deliberately considered and designed to address its special architectural and visual qualities. In this regard the benefits to the Old Town Conservation Area that will be derived from the implementation of the Caltongate Development Project will vastly outweigh the impact of necessary beneficial change.

Executive summary

The heritage case for the Caltongate Development was, by necessity, expansive. I have incorporated below the text of the executive summary, intended to distill the overall case for the consumption of key decision-makers. The section references are to the individual chapters of the Heritage Statement:

The Caltongate master plan

The Caltongate master plan was approved by the City of Edinburgh Council on 5 October 2006 on the basis of an extensive formal consultation exercise. It provides supplementary planning guidance within the context of the development control process.

The Caltongate master plan has been prepared by the Council to guide the redevelopment of a series of sites within the Waverley Valley, collectively known as 'Caltongate' for the purpose of the master plan. It includes land at East Market Street, New Street, Calton Road and Canongate.

It expands upon existing specific policy and guidelines set out in the Waverley Valley Redevelopment Strategy by acknowledging the necessity, both economically and architecturally, of reconnecting the area requiring regeneration into the wider city fabric. Indeed it acknowledges that the regeneration of this specific area presents a significant opportunity to improve the connections between Holyrood and the New Town.

In so doing it also acknowledges that the physical impact of any regeneration proposals will extend into the existing built fabric of the Old Town.

The aspirations of the Caltongate master plan

The aspirations of the Caltongate master plan can be summarised as follows:

1. to bring increased population, related local services and a mix of uses to the area;
2. to create new streets and spaces that establish new urban connections through the Valley that will encourage ease of movement and generate activity within the Old Town by increasing frontage and unlocking the potential of development sites;

3. to create a major new public square – fitting in with a growing family of public spaces off the Royal Mile – offering the means to regenerate Canongate and bring an additional focus and destination;

4. to create new buildings and spaces of the highest architectural and urban design quality that conserve and reinforce the existing historic and landscape context.

The benefits that it is envisaged will be derived from the implementation of the master plan correspond to these aspirations.

The Caltongate Development Project

The Caltongate Development Project consists of the following development proposals, which in combination will implement the Caltongate master plan.

PA 1 Caltongate North – Erection of buildings for affordable housing (flats), use of ground floor for community facility (drop-in centre) and alternative retail (Class 1), financial, professional or other services (Class 2) and/or business (Class 4) purposes. Alterations to steps and boundary wall of Calton Hill Stairs.

PA 2 Caltongate Central – Enabling works including erection of podium structure, installation of ground source heating system and associated work.

PA 3 Caltongate Central – Erection of buildings for use as offices, retail (Class 1), restaurant and/or bar, business (Class 4) premises, podium structure (including ground source heating), car parking, access and public square.

PA 4 Caltongate Central – Erection of buildings for use as residential, retail (Class 1), restaurant and/or bar, business (Class 4) premises, podium structure, car parking, access and public square.

PA 5 Caltongate Central – Redevelopment and erection of buildings, with part retained façades, for use as hotel, retail (Class 1), restaurant and/or bar, car parking, access, servicing area and public square.

PA 6 Caltongate West – Redevelopment and erection of buildings for use as residential/business (live/work) units, affordable housing (flats), offices, retail (Class 1), access and servicing area. Realignment of Cranston Street.

PA 7 Caltongate West – Redevelopment and erection of buildings for use as offices, retail (Class 1), restaurant and/or bar, entertainment premises, with access and open area, and alternative use of arches for retail (Class 1), restaurant and/or bar, showroom and/or business (Class 4) purposes. Realignment of Cranston Street.

Development proposals

The detailed proposals are presented in the drawings and documents supporting the applications for planning permission and listed building and conservation area consent submitted to the City of Edinburgh Council.

Essential components

The economic and architectural feasibility of the Caltongate Development Project is reliant upon the following essential component parts, without which it will not be possible to develop the overall site in the manner envisaged under the Caltongate master plan:

- The connection into the Canongate;
- The specific provision of a five-star hotel and conference centre;
- The activation of East Market Street.

The design of these essential components has evolved through the master plan process and beyond. The means by which resultant impacts have been minimised through design is discussed within the main text. It is acknowledged that these essential component parts are the aspects of the project that will have the most significant localised impacts upon the existing built heritage.

Heritage issues

Regarding heritage issues, the Caltongate master plan generally reiterates existing local and national policy. However, it specifically acknowledges that there may be circumstances where a case can be made that the wider beneficial regenerative nature of the master plan will outweigh negative impact upon the existing historic fabric.

It also emphasises design quality as a principal factor in the consideration of applications for planning, listed building and conservation consent. In this regard, it reflects the guidance provided in NPPG 18 and the Memorandum of Guidance. It also reflects the comments made in Historic Scotland's consultation response during the master plan process.

Benefits

The social, economic and cultural benefits that will be derived from the implementation of the master plan are summarised and discussed within the main text. In broad terms the specific cultural or heritage benefits are:

a) the enhancement of the character and appearance of the Old Town Conservation Area and the Old and New Towns of Edinburgh World Heritage Site by regenerating a significant, presently semi-derelict part of these areas;

b) the proper re-connection of the re-emerging Canongate and Holyrood with the wider city;

c) the re-vitalisation of the Canongate, by the introduction of new uses that will activate the street, and the consequent enhancement of its character and appearance as part of the Royal Mile;

d) the development of the Category C(S) Listed Jeffrey Street Arches in sustainable use, on the basis of their interrelationship with the new district;

e) the replacement of existing utilitarian piecemeal development along East Market Street with a specifically integrated urban street, with all the opportunities this creates for new 'traditional' connections between the Canongate and Market Street, in the form of wynds and closes;

f) the improved sightlines and connectivity between the Canongate and Calton Hill, including new or improved framed views towards the monuments on Calton Hill, and consequently the improved presentation of the historic built environment in these areas;

g) The improved prospects for the maintenance of the existing historic built fabric on the basis of the improved economic environment.

h) Specifically, the improved prospects for the sustainable ongoing use of Category B Listed Milton House Primary School on the Canongate.

i) The improved prospects for the further sympathetic regeneration of the Canongate between the Canongate Parish Church and Holyrood. This is any area where a number of distinctly dreary utilitarian buildings have been introduced in the late 20th century.

j) the reintroduction of traditional paving and other materials under the public realm improvements proposed.

Design quality

The developer has been committed to design of the highest quality from the outset. This is reflected in his choice of Architects and the consultative process that has helped inform the evolution of the Caltongate Development Project.

The design of the overall scheme and the individual development proposals has been guided by the principles set out in the Caltongate master plan and the contextual analysis of the overall and individual sites. This contextual approach has minimised the impact of the overall development on the existing built heritage.

In this regard the quality of the proposals specifically addresses guidance set out within NPPG 18 and the Memorandum of Guidance.

Assessment of impacts

The following impacts on the existing historic built fabric have been assessed in terms of NPPG 18 and the Memorandum of Guidance, and in terms of the Caltongate master plan within the main text.

A. Impact on Listed Buildings

a) The partial demolition of the Category C(S) Listed Old Sailor's Ark.

b) The demolition of the Category C(S) Listed Canongate Venture (5 New Street).

c) The alterations to the Category C(S) Listed wall, vaults, railings and pier at Jeffrey Street.

d) The minor alterations to the Category B Listed north gable wall of 12–18 Jeffrey Street and 7–9 Cranston Street.

e)   The impacts on the settings of various Listed Buildings and structures on the Canongate, Jeffrey Street, Regent's Road and Calton Hill, adjacent the master plan area.

B. Impact on Conservation Area

f)   The demolition with part retained façades of unlisted 1930s tenements (221–229 Canongate) to enable the connection of 'Parliament Way' into the Canongate, and the creation of a new five-star hotel on the Canongate.

g)   The demolition of the former Car Depot in East Market Street, in order to bring otherwise 'sterilised' runs of Market Street and New Street frontage into viable street level use.

h)   The demolition of 20 Calton Road.

i)   The impacts upon what are considered to be the essential characteristics of the Old Town Conservation Area.

C. Impact on World Heritage Site

j)   The impacts upon what are considered to be the features of universal value within the Old and New Towns of Edinburgh World Heritage Site.

Conclusions

It is acknowledged that the Caltongate Development Project will have a physical impact upon the existing built environment that extends beyond the regeneration of the site centred on the now demolished former Bus Garage. This will however be limited to what is necessary to ensure the sustainability of the regeneration project and its successful integration within the wider fabric of the city.

The design of the overall scheme and the individual development proposals has been guided by the principles set out in the Caltongate master plan and the contextual analysis of the sites. This contextual approach taken with the extensive consultation that has taken place throughout both the master plan and pre-planning process has both minimised the impact of the overall development on what is important to the existing built heritage and resolved existing incongruities.

In terms of the tests set in NPPG 18 and the Memorandum of Guidance, it is considered that the quality of the development proposals coupled with the social, economic and cultural benefits that will be derived from the completed project will vastly outweigh the limited physical impact upon what is genuinely important within the existing historic fabric.

Regarding the Old Town and New Town Conservation Areas, and the Old and New Towns of Edinburgh World Heritage Site, on balance, the benefits that will be derived from the implementation of the Caltongate Development Project, coupled with the quality of its contextual design, will vastly outweigh the impact of necessary change. It is considered that the Caltongate Development Project will enhance the character and appearance of both Conservation Areas and will protect the genuinely outstanding universal values of the World Heritage Site whilst promoting its harmonious adaptation to the needs of contemporary life in a modern city.

Summary

It can be seen from the above extracts that the essential basis for the cases for Listed Building and Conservation Area consent relating to the Caltongate Development Proposal was that the benefits that were to be derived from the proposal would significantly outweigh the specifically minimized impacts on the existing built heritage.

In terms of the Planning (Listed Buildings and Conservation Areas) (Scotland) Act 1997, consideration of the case made within the Heritage Statement was held to demonstrate that special regard to the desirability of preserving Listed Buildings and their settings (or any features of special architectural or historic interest that they possessed) and special attention to the desirability of preserving or enhancing the character or appearance of that area had been paid on the part of all the relevant decision-making bodies.

Case Study 2

Former Notre Dame Campus, Bearsden, near Glasgow

Introduction

2.1
Aerial view of former Notre Dame Campus, *c.*2000 (courtesy of East Dunbartonshire Council)

Regeneration of the former Notre Dame Campus site at Bearsden, near Glasgow, commenced with the site being split to create a suitably sized area of land for a new secondary school, with the remainder, which is dominated by a 1960s, Category A listed, former dormitory complex, being set aside as a commercial redevelopment opportunity that was intended, in part, to contribute to the overall funding of the new school (Figures 2.1–2.3).

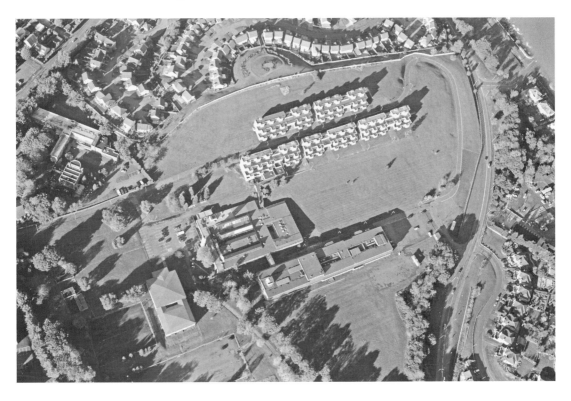

2.2
Aerial view of former Notre Dame Campus, *c.*2000 (courtesy of East Dunbartonshire Council)

2.3
Listed Buildings, former Notre Dame Campus © Crown Copyright and/or database right. All rights reserved. Licence number 100049743

The technical difficulties and costs associated with redeveloping the existing Listed Buildings to an appropriate alternative use vastly outweigh their commercial value. Consequently, the buildings can realistically never be brought back into a viable use.

This was a more recent case than Caltongate and is based on the guidance provided in SHEP and SPP 23 (October 2008). As it essentially focuses on a single issue, I have incorporated below, accompanied by commentary where appropriate, more or less the complete Heritage Statement submitted in support of the applications for Planning and Listed Building consent. These were approved by the local authority in October 2009.

Pre-application discussion

Prior to the application for Planning and Listed Building consent eventually being submitted, the case for Listed Building consent was presented in draft and discussed first of all with the local authority and thereafter with both the local authority and Historic Scotland. As part of these discussions it was agreed that an outline planning application with specific detailed information would be an appropriate vehicle for applying for Listed Building consent.

Heritage Statement

The supporting Heritage Statement presented the case for Listed Building consent.

General background

A general background was provided that concluded with the then current planning situation:

General background

Gillespie, Kidd & Coia

Gillespie, Kidd & Coia were commissioned by the Board of Governors to design the Notre Dame College Campus in the early 1960s. In this respect the RC Archdiocese of Glasgow had been a principal Client of Gillespie, Kidd & Coia from the 1930s. From the mid–1950s the design work of the practice was generally led by Izi Metzstein and Andrew MacMillan, and essentially followed an idiosyncratic international modernist idiom.

At the time of instruction the practice had recently completed or were working on the following major projects:

1959–1966	St Peter's Seminary, Cardross
1959	Maternity Hospital, Bellshill
1958–1962	Kildrum Primary School, Cumbernauld
1961–1963	Howford School, 531 Crookston Road, Glasgow, G53 7TX
1962–1965	St Benedict's RC Church, Easterhouse
1963–1964	Our Lady's RC High School, Cumbernauld
1963–1964	St Bride's RC Church, East Kilbride
1963–1967	University of Hull, Halls of Residence
1964	Round Riding Road Housing, Dumbarton
1964	Sacred Heart RC Church, Cumbernauld
1964	St Patrick's RC Church, Kilsyth
1965	Our Lady of Good Counsel RC Church, Dennistoun, Glasgow

Site

On the west of the proposed site for the college campus was the original St Peter's Seminary (which had been relocated to an outstanding new modernist campus, designed by MacMillan and Metzstein, at Cardross). The remainder of the site sloped up from the area of relatively flat land adjacent the Stockiemuir Road up to a high point known as Hungry Hill (Figure 2.4).

Design

The design produced by Gillespie, Kidd and Coia juxtaposed the administration, teaching blocks and residential halls in a nominal eastward facing open courtyard arrangement. The single aspect residential halls stepping in two rows down the south facing slope formed the north side of the 'court', with the administration and teaching blocks forming the west and south sides of the 'court', respectively (Figures 2.1, 2.2 and 2.5).

Other buildings belonging to the original design of the campus included a gymnasium block to the west of the administration block, and

2.4
Extract from 1964 OS map © Crown Copyright and/or database right. All rights reserved. Licence number 100049743

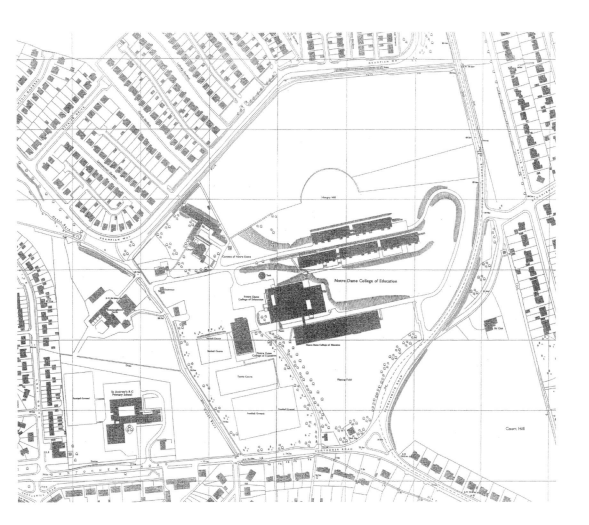

gatehouses at the western and southern access points to the site. Playing fields and sports courts were located to the south and west of the gymnasium and to the south of the teaching block.

The unique forms of the residence halls and their prominent hillside location have lent a higher level of importance to these buildings than might usually have been afforded them within the context of a college campus. Contemporary design influences might have included the Ziggurat Halls of Residence at the University of East Anglia, by Sir Denys Lasdun, which had been completed around 1962, and Habitat at the 1967 Expo in Montreal, by Moshe Safdie, although neither utilised a hillside context in the same manner.

The principal buildings, the teaching and administration blocks, were less stylized concrete framed structures that firmly rooted the residential halls within a clearly defined campus context (Figures 2.1 and 2.2).

Contemporary drawings indicate that further residential blocks were contemplated further down the slope.

The original campus was completed around 1969 and, in overall form, changed little prior to its eventual closure in 2002, although a number of material alterations were made during this period to address technical problems; most evident of these was the replacement of the original smooth concrete render with a pebble-dash render (Figures 2.6–2.13).

2.6
General view of dormitory block (courtesy of Hurd Rolland Partnership)

2.7
General view along Spine Road (courtesy of Hurd Rolland Partnership)

2.8
General view of dormitory block (courtesy of Hurd Rolland Partnership)

2.9
General view of dormitory block adjacent Spine Road (courtesy of Hurd Rolland Partnership)

2.10
General view of rear
of dormitory block
(courtesy of Hurd
Rolland Partnership)

2.11
Rear entrance to
dormitory block
(courtesy of Hurd
Rolland Partnership)

2.12
Close-up showing deteriorating condition (courtesy of Hurd Rolland Partnership)

2.13
Close-up showing deteriorating condition (courtesy of Hurd Rolland Partnership)

Local context

The original campus was deliberately secluded from its wider local context. In this respect it provided a blank canvas for its strictly modernist architecture. During the intervening years, suburban housing has encroached more and more on its boundaries (Figures 2.5 and 2.14). An unfortunate by-product of its present semi-derelict condition and its uncompromising modern design is that the now deteriorating complex has taken on the appearance of a run down, new-town council estate, and in this respect is entirely incongruous with the local character of this part of Bearsden (Figures 2.6–2.10).

Decline

Notre Dame College merged with Roman Catholic Craiglockart College in 1981 to form St Andrew's College of Education, the only national Catholic college of education in Scotland. Thereafter it gradually merged with Glasgow University, becoming part of the University's Faculty of Education from 1999. Under this gradual process the Bearsden campus became surplus to requirement in 1998 and was eventually vacated in 2002.

Historic Scotland Listing

Historic Scotland Category A listed the residence blocks on 4 March 1998. Strangely, whilst referring to the other buildings on the campus, within the information published by Historic Scotland there was no recognition that

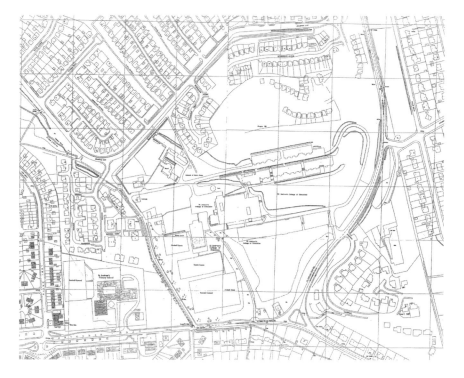

2.14
Extract from 1995 OS map © Crown Copyright and/or database right. All rights reserved. Licence number 100049743

the residence blocks, in form and function, were inextricably part of the wider design.

Current planning situation

Subsequent to a series of planning applications since 2002, the original site has become subdivided under the current PFI scheme to construct the new Bearsden Academy. This has seen the demolition of all of the unlisted buildings of the original campus to enable the construction of the new school premises on the western part of the site, and has left the remainder of the original site, which includes the redundant and semi-derelict residential blocks, to be regenerated separately . . .

Under the outline planning application for the overall site, granted by the Scottish Ministers in December 2005, the demolition of the two uppermost residential blocks (and all of the unlisted buildings) was approved in principle, largely in acknowledgement that the wholesale retention of these buildings was neither practical nor commercially viable within the context of the master plan for the wider site.

Subsequent to the subdivision of the site, all attempts to develop a practical and commercially viable scheme for the easternmost part have failed due to the limited land available for new development (and consequently cross-funding) and the prohibitive costs involved in re-using the listed residential blocks. In correspondence and informal consultation Historic Scotland continues to accept the loss of the two uppermost blocks should this be necessary. However, all financial appraisals indicate that the retention of any of the residential blocks is effectively blighting the remaining site and that for successful regeneration to take place the loss of all of these buildings, whilst regrettable, will be necessary . . .

In this regard the developer is seeking to devise a state of the art regeneration proposal that will replace the remaining semi-derelict buildings with a scheme that meets as many of the local authority's aspirations for the site as possible and is designed to highest contemporary architectural and environmental standards.

Relevant policy and guidance

The key relevant policy upon which the justification for demolition would be based was then set out:

Relevant policy and guidance

Planning (Listed Buildings and Conservation Areas) (Scotland) Act 1997

The principal statutory requirements regarding the demolition of listed buildings is set out in the Planning (Listed Buildings and Conservation Areas) (Scotland) Act 1997:

General duty as respects listed buildings in exercise of planning functions

59(1) In considering whether to grant planning permission for development which affects a listed building or its setting, a planning authority or the Secretary of State [the Scottish Ministers], as the case may be, shall have special regard to the desirability of preserving the building or its setting or any features of special architectural or historic interest which it possesses.

Decision on application

14(2) In considering whether to grant listed building consent for any works, the planning authority or the Secretary of State [the Scottish Ministers], as the case may be, shall have special regard to the desirability of preserving the building or its setting or any features of special architectural or historic interest which it possesses.

In this regard the Act does not preclude the demolition of a Listed Building, rather it directs the relevant authority to the desirability of preserving such structures and that special regard should be taken of this when making planning decisions.

SPP 23: Planning and the Historic Environment

Regarding the demolition of Listed Buildings and Structures, SPP 23 provides a model policy at Annexe A, stating:

MODEL POLICY 1: Listed Buildings

. . . There is a presumption against demolition or other works that adversely affect the special interest of a listed building or its setting.

No listed buildings should be demolished unless it can be clearly demonstrated that:

- the building is not of special interest; or
- the building is incapable of repair; or
- the demolition of the building is essential to delivering significant benefits to economic growth or the wider community; or
- the repair of the building is not economically viable and that it has been marketed at a price reflecting its location and condition to potential restoring purchasers for a reasonable period.

RCAHMS shall be formally notified of all proposals to demolish listed buildings to enable features to be recorded.

Model Policy 1 effectively replaces the tests previously identified within the Memorandum of Guidance. In this respect, it should be noted that whilst the earlier tests are essentially re-applied there is now a stand alone test stating 'no listed building should be demolished unless it can be clearly demonstrated that the demolition of the building is essential to delivering significant benefits to economic growth or the wider community economic growth'. In this regard at paragraph 36 of SPP 23 the potential benefits to be derived from the re-use or regeneration of a historically sensitive site is afforded specific significance within the decision-making process:

> Scottish Ministers' policies on listed building consent and on the considerations to be taken account by planning authorities in determining listed building consent applications for alteration, adaptation or demolition of a listed building are set out in the current SHEP.

Scottish Historic Environment Policy – October 2008 (SHEP)

Under the heading 'Listed Building Consent', SHEP states:

> **Applications**
>
> 3.44 Knowing what is important about a building is central to an understanding of how to protect its special interest. Applications should demonstrate that, in arriving at a strategy for intervention, the importance of the building has been clearly understood and those features which contribute to its special interest have been identified.
>
> 3.45 In general, the more extensive the intervention which is proposed, the more supporting information applications should provide. Where proposals involve significant intervention, evidence that less intrusive options have been considered should be provided. Where the application would have a significantly adverse effect on the building's special interest, but is believed to offer significant benefits to economic growth or the wider community, applicants should prepare a statement which justifies the intervention in relation to these benefits. This statement should demonstrate that the benefits could not be realised without the intervention proposed.

Regarding determination of an application for the demolition of a Listed Building SHEP states:

> 3.52 In the case of applications for the demolition of listed buildings it is Scottish Ministers' policy that no listed building should be demolished unless it can be clearly demonstrated that every effort has been made to retain it. Planning authorities should therefore only approve such applications where they are satisfied that:
>
> a.   the building is not of special interest; or
> b.   the building is incapable of repair; or

c.   the demolition of the building is essential to delivering signi-
    ficant benefits to economic growth or the wider community;
    or

d.   the repair of the building is not economically viable and that
    it has been marketed at a price reflecting its location and
    condition to potential restoring purchasers for a reasonable
    period.

Glasgow and Clyde Valley Joint Structure Plan and East Dunbartonshire Local Plan

Regarding the demolition of Listed Buildings, Glasgow and Clyde Valley
Joint Structure Plan and the East Dunbartonshire Local Plan essentially
reflect national policy. At present, the wording of the Local Plan remains
in line with previous national policy documents, NPPG 18 and the
Memorandum of Guidance.

Conclusion

Whilst there is a requirement to have special regard to the desirability of
preserving a listed building it is acknowledged that a case for demolition
can be made on the basis that:

- the building is not of special interest; or
- the building is incapable of repair; or
- the demolition of the building is essential to delivering significant
  benefits to economic growth or the wider community; or
- the repair of the building is not economically viable and that it has
  been marketed at a price reflecting its location and condition to
  potential restoring purchasers for a reasonable period.

In terms of current policy and guidance the principal justification for the
proposed demolition of the Residence Halls is that:

- The repair of the building in its present or alternative use is not
  practically or economically viable.
- The demolition of the building is essential to delivering significant
  benefits to economic growth or the wider community that will be
  derived from the regeneration of the overall site.

The diminished special interest and present material and structural
condition of the Listed Buildings are considered to be mitigating factors.
        These are discussed in the following order in Part 2 of this
Report:

- Special interest
- Material and structural condition
- Viability of the remaining buildings
- Benefits of regeneration.

Special interest

Although special interest was not a principal justification for the proposed demolition, the diminution of this interest was identified as a significant mitigating factor that required to be taken into consideration:

Special interest

Introduction

The Residence Halls at St Andrew's College were Category A Listed on 4 March 1998. The special interest of these buildings, in terms of relevant current policy and guidance is considered within this section.

Categories of Listing

SHEP states (at Note 2.19):

> Listed buildings are given categories of listing which distinguish their relative merit. These categories have no statutory weight but are advisory. They inform levels of designation and grant award. There are three categories, defined as follows:
>
> A   buildings of national or international importance, either architectural or historic, or fine, little-altered examples of some particular period style or building type;
>
> B   buildings of regional or more than local importance, or major examples of some particular period, style or building type;
>
> C(S) buildings of local importance; lesser examples of any period, style, or building type, as originally constructed or altered; and simple, traditional buildings which group well with others.
>
> In addition, a system of group categories exists to highlight the contextual relationship which an individual listed building may possess in relation to others. These are A and B Groups. They are in addition to the individual category and likewise have no statutory significance. They serve to flag considerations of setting, function, design, planning and historic combinations where the individual value is enhanced by its association with others.

Criteria for determining whether a building is of 'special architectural or historic interest'

Annexe 2 to SHEP sets out the Criteria for determining whether a building is of 'special architectural or historic interest':

1.   The criteria can only provide a framework within which professional judgement is exercised in reaching individual decisions.
2.   To be listed, a building need not be functioning for the purpose originally intended. For example, a redundant railway viaduct may have continued its life as a walkway or cycle path, even a wildlife sanctuary.

3. The principles of selection for statutory listing are broadly:

   a. age and rarity;

   b. architectural or historic interest;

   c. close historical associations.

Relevant to the Residence Halls at Bearsden in relation to Age and Rarity, Annexe 2 states:

4. The older a building is and the fewer of its type that survive the more likely it is to present a special interest. Age is a major factor in the evaluation process but its weight differs across the building types. Period definitions are given to facilitate the assessment but these are not intended to be watersheds or cut-off points . . .

7. Those erected after 1945 may merit inclusion on the lists if their special architectural or historic interest is of definite architectural quality . . .

Of particular relevance in relation to Architectural or Historic Interest, it notes:

9. Selection for architectural or historic interest is assessed under a range of broad headings, summarised below . . .

13. Setting: The context in which a structure sits can be a critical factor in its evaluation. It invariably accounts for its form and should not be under-rated. A structure whose setting has changed adversely, removing the original contextual character, or which has been removed from its context, has one less factor in support of its case for designation.

The criteria for listing under the heading 'Close Historical Associations' are not relevant in this instance where the listing essentially relates to architectural significance.

Under the updated guidance there is no reference to 'the work of a well known architect' as a criterion for listing.

Under the heading 'Working with the Principles' Annexe 2 states:

16. In choosing buildings within the above broad principles:

   a. particular attention is paid to the special value within building types, either for architectural or planning reasons, or as illustrating social and economic history;

   b. a building may be listed for its contribution to an architecturally or historically interesting group, such as a planned burgh, town square or model village as well as its intrinsic merit considered in isolation;

   c. the impact of vernacular buildings in particular is often made not only by individual buildings but by their grouping. At the other end of the spectrum, a major country house may well be enhanced by adjacent buildings such as stables, lodges, gatepiers and bridges in its curtilage, and vice versa;

d. authenticity, that is a building's closeness to the original fabric and therefore its ability to convey its significance, and levels of integrity, carries weight. It need not be the case that a building is as originally built, because changes made to it may have added to its significance. What is added or taken away will be considered for the overall benefit or detriment to its character.

Annexe 2 concludes by noting:

17. It is important to stress that when buildings are being considered for listing, no factors other than architectural or historic interest as defined above can be taken into account. The condition of a property, for example, is not a factor in the evaluation unless it detracts significantly from the architectural or historic interest so that it can no longer be defined as special.

Information supplementary to the Statutory List

The description published by Historic Scotland in relation to the statutory listing of the Residence Halls stated:

Description:

Gillespie, Kidd and Coia, 1968–9. 5 blocks of 3-storey (double height), 13-bay stepped cubic residential halls (Ogilvie House, Consuela Hall, Eyre Hall, Lescher Hall and Julie Billiart Hall) with alternating advanced/recessed bays. Harl. Ogilvie House, Consuela Hall and Eyre Hall lie horizonally aligned to S, Julie Billiart and Lescher Hall lie horizontally aligned to their N. Steps flank Consuela Hall and divide Julie Billiart and Lescher Hall.

S (ENTRANCE) ELEVATION, EYRE HALL: grouped 7–1–5. Steps to recessed double-width near-central glass entrance; timber and glass door to re-entrant angle to right; advanced double-width bay above. Pattern of recessed and advanced bays (cantilever to central upper storey) to remaining bays. Double-width bays to recessed 3rd, 5th and 11th bays.

CONSUELA HALL: grouped 5–1–7. Pattern as above, with double-width bays to 3rd, 9th and 11th bays.

OGILVIE HOUSE: grouped 7–1–5. Pattern as above, with double-width bays to 3rd, 5th and 11th bays. Modern extension to entrance links block with administration building to S.

LESCHER HALL: grouped 7–1–5. Pattern as above, with double-width bays to 3rd, 5th and 11th bays.

JULIE BILLIART HALL: grouped 7–1–5. Pattern as above, with double-width bays to 3rd, 5th and 11th bays.

N (REAR ELEVATION), EYRE HALL: recessed 2-leaf timber and glass door left of centre; timber door to left. Steps to 2 boarded stair towers to left, 3 to right; timber and glass door. Single clerestory strips flanking doorway (double strip to right) and to outer right and left; double strips between stair towers.

CONSUELA HALL: Eyre Hall pattern reversed.

OGILVIE HOUSE, LESCHER HALL AND JULIE BILLIART HALL: as Eyre Hall. (Walkways to Ogilvie House.) Fixed plate glass and casement windows (some louvres). Flat roof; copper roof to main entrance of each block.

INTERIOR: timber and patterned glass to communal area; timber floor; timber screening to staircases.

The supplementary information continued by noting:

Notes:

Formerly known as Notre Dame College. Also on the site designed by Gillespie, Kidd and Coia are 2 teaching blocks and a physical education building. The campus draws much of its inspiration from the 'Shakespearean Seven' new universities of the 1960s: Sussex, York, East Anglia, Kent, Essex, Warwick and Lancaster, all built on greenfield sites. The most dominant influence being the University of East Anglia (begun 1962, by Sir Denys Lasdun) with its stepped hillside siting of cubic student accommodation. An important point of interest at Bearsden lies in the architectural emphasis on the student residences rather than the more common emphasis on teaching blocks found in post war university building (for example, Stirling and Gowan's Engineering Building, Leicester University, 1959–63). In this sense, the halls of residence contribute to a wider scheme of social relations, most notably those of Le Corbusier's Unite principles of an alternative city with an ideal harmony of man, nature and urban existence.

Assessment

The special interest of the Notre Dame College Campus relates to the following:

1. As a campus, it was one of a number of architectural projects undertaken by Gillespie, Kidd and Coia when that practice was at the height of its modernist renown.
2. In their original condition, the Residence Halls, in particular, provided a distinctive example of modern functionalist architecture derived from a readily identifiable mix of contemporary influences and the specific sloping context of the site.

Overall campus

Strangely, the listing of the campus only mentioned the five Residence Halls. This specifically ignored the fact that these were an interdependent part of a wider campus design that provided their essential physical and functional context.

The subsequent demolition of the Administration and Teaching Blocks has stripped away a significant part of the essential original context of the Residence Halls leaving only what remains of their own inherent original value.

Individual Residence Halls

The Residence Halls were of relatively low specification – felt roofing, smooth cement render subsequently replaced in slip shod fashion by a locally more traditional pebble dash finish, timber single-glazed windows – and suffered from poor attention to technical and in some instances architectural detailing (Figures 2.6–2.13). Their anticipated life cycle might have been in the region of 25–40 years (which appears to have corresponded to the actual functional life of the buildings). Consequently, whilst, in terms of contemporary modern architectural influences and their site generated form, they are buildings of some architectural significance, they are not of the highest material or technical quality.

The current poor appearance of the buildings reflects this relatively low material specification to the extent that it 'detracts significantly from their architectural interest.'

Historic Scotland Listing

All of the above calls into question their present Category A Listing. Whereas, at the time of their listing, they might genuinely have had a special interest as part of a 'little-altered' campus 'of national or international importance', in terms of relevant national guidance, with the subsequent removal of, particularly, the Administration and Teaching Blocks, the original context has been 'changed adversely, removing the original contextual character' and consequently 'has one less factor in support of its case . . .'.

Taken in conjunction with the principle that 'those erected after 1945 may merit inclusion on the lists if their special architectural or historic interest is of definite architectural quality . . .', it should be considered that, notwithstanding their inherently unusual architectural form, the special interest of these buildings has been significantly diminished.

Mitigation

In mitigation to the potential loss of these buildings, there are a number of other extant and more sustainable examples of the work of Gillespie Kidd & Coia from this period.

Date	Project	Listing category
1959–1966	St Peter's Seminary, Cardross (severely dilapidated)	A
1958–1962	Kildrum Primary School, Cumbernauld	B
1963–1964	Our Lady's RC High School, Cumbernauld	B
1963–1964	St Bride's RC Church, East Kilbride	A
1963–1967	University of Hull, Halls of Residence	Presently Unlisted
1964	Sacred Heart RC Church, Cumbernauld	A
1964	St Patrick's RC Church, Kilsyth	A
1972–1975	Cumbernauld Technical College, Cumbernauld	B
1974	Robinson College, Cambridge	Presently Unlisted

Condition

The Heritage Statement then continued with the assessment of Condition, which was a considerable issue, but again not the principal justification for demolition:

Material and structural condition

Introduction

The residential blocks are currently in a semi-derelict condition, to the extent that access into the interior of the buildings is no longer readily available. In this regard reference should be made to the separate reports prepared by the architect and the structural engineer.

Original detail design

Due in part to the innovative nature of the design, the multitude of parapeted flat felt roofs, the initial use of flat cement render, the extensive cold bridging, and the lack of sufficient cross-ventilation (Figures 2.6–2.13), problems with water ingress and condensation were experienced in these buildings virtually from the outset.

The originally specified cement render was replaced, not entirely successfully, by a pebble dash render to address the essentially inappropriate nature of the former specification within the context of the local Scottish climate (Figures 2.6–2.13).

Alterations to the windows to address the ventilation and condensation issues were undertaken in 1978, at the same time as (largely utilitarian) works were being undertaken to meet the then current fire regulations (Figures 2.6–2.13).

Current material condition

The Residential Blocks have now lain empty for a considerable period and with only minimal maintenance being undertaken and the occurrence of theft and vandalism, the building fabric is in a very poor state of repair.

There is evidence of rotting window frames, discolouration and cracking to the pebble dash render, water ingress through poorly maintained or vandalised roofs and windows (Figures 2.6–2.13).

Notwithstanding that security arrangements were put in place by East Dunbartonshire Council, there has almost inevitably been wholesale theft of copper roof coverings and any other salvageable materials (Figures 2.6–2.13).

All of which, taken in conjunction with the inherently poor original detailing of the buildings, has led to the present situation where there is manifest rot and mould growth and the general deterioration of the building fabric throughout the remaining complex.

Structural condition

Notwithstanding their very poor material condition, the buildings are considered to be structurally viable.

Repair and maintenance costs

The costs of undertaking the repairs and maintenance necessary to return the buildings to a maintainable shell state will be in the region of £2 million. These are set out in the separate report prepared by the Quantity Surveyor and include for the extensive repairs and maintenance required to the roofs, windows and render and the removal of mould growth and water damage internally. They also make an allowance for trace heating and the security of the buildings.

In terms of the tests set out in SHEP, it is considered that the buildings are technically not 'incapable of repair', but that their repair 'is not economically viable'.

Viability of the remaining buildings

Viability was a principal justification for demolition. In this regard, the provision of development options, cost information and development appraisals became the central tools for demonstrating that the buildings would essentially never be capable of being brought back into viable use:

Viability of the remaining buildings proposals

A detailed scheme for the alternative use of some of the remaining residence blocks was prepared. This was developed on the basis of the outline planning approval obtained in December 2005 and, consequently, upon the assumption that the demolition of the two rear residential blocks would create a situation where the retention of the three front blocks would be viable and cross-fundable from the wider redevelopment of the eastern part of the site.

It should be noted that the scheme required a level of associated new build development that under normal circumstances would have been considered to be a substantial overdevelopment of the site.

In this respect the scheme was tacitly supported by Historic Scotland.

Practical requirements to meet current Building Regulations and modern spatial requirements

The architect's report on Listed Hostels at the former Notre Dame Campus site sets out the significant practical requirements associated with meeting current Building Regulations requirements. In summary these include:

- necessary alterations to the external walls to achieve current insulation requirements;
- necessary alterations to internal walls to achieve current sound insulation and fire performance requirements;
- replacement of the roofs in their entirety to meet current insulation requirements;
- replacement of existing windows to meet current insulation, fire escape and cleaning standards;
- replacement of the ground floor to meet current insulation and sub floor ventilation requirements;
- necessary alterations to the upper floors to meet current acoustic requirements;
- additional flues and extract fans to kitchens and toilets to meet current ventilation requirements;
- installation of cavity barriers to meet fire regulations;
- relaxation of fire escape and fire access requirements;
- relaxation of DDA requirements;
- relaxation of enhanced apartment requirement;
- relaxation of requirement to have a toilet on each principle floor.

The above requirements would be the minimum necessary to return the buildings to their original use as a particularly basic form of cellular student accommodation with limited communal facilities. This use is no longer required, and conversion to some form of modern residential use provides the only realistic opportunity regarding their viable future use. The Architect's report sets out the significant practical difficulties that arise in attempting to meet any acceptable spatial configuration for modern residential use. In summary these include:

- Lack of large spaces suited to conversion to modern essentially open plan requirements.
- Limited floor to ceiling heights.
- Poor levels of daylighting and ventilation.
- Poor visual amenity from many of the existing rooms.
- Privacy issues at ground floor rooms.

The significant structural and material alterations necessary to address these issues are discussed in both the architect's and structural engineer's reports.

The report prepared by the quantity surveyor indicates that taking into account the above constraints, the estimated cost for converting the hostels will be in the region of £175 per square foot, around 75 per cent higher than might normally be anticipated for a development involving the conversion of existing buildings.

In real terms the quantity surveyor's cost appraisal envisages a present construction cost of £9.4 million for the conversion of the existing buildings, which requires to be set against a revenue of £7.6 million. This deficit would require to be cross-funded from new build development elsewhere on the site.

Development appraisals

Detailed development appraisals for the overall eastern part of the site have been undertaken which assess various permutations of these proposals in an attempt to establish the commercial viability of the site on the basis of retaining three out of five of the remaining listed buildings. These are confidential but will be made available to those responsible for scrutinising the application. In summary the appraisals project the following headline figures:

	Form of development	Date	Projected profit (loss)	Yield (%)
Appraisal 1	Mixed	2007	£72,000	0.22
Appraisal 2	Mixed	2009	(£8,500,000)	(26.7)
Appraisal 3	Residential	2007	£7,000,000	13.4
Appraisal 4	Residential	2009	(£18,500,000)	(31)

Appraisal 3 reflects the previously developed proposal. It can be seen that, even in 2007, with a substantial new build element, this was a marginal scheme in terms of development yield. Increased on-costs and the changed economic climate have created a situation where regeneration of the site, with the listed buildings remaining, even with an excessive new build element, is just not tenable.

Benefits of regeneration

The principal mitigation for the demolition of the buildings, the benefits that would accrue from the regeneration of the site, was set out within the remaining section of the Heritage Statement:

Benefits of regeneration

Introduction

SHEP states:

> ... no listed building should be demolished unless it can be clearly demonstrated that every effort has been made to retain it. Planning authorities should therefore only approve such applications where they are satisfied that ... the demolition of the building is essential to delivering significant benefits to economic growth or the wider community ...

Local policy

Existing local and regional aspirations for the site provide a useful baseline regarding the benefits to economic growth and to the wider community foreseen for its regeneration. This is discussed at length within the separate planning report but in summary includes:

- Under the GCVJSP provision of new business land on an identified suburban brownfield site.
- Integration of new development to the benefit of existing communities.
- Under UC 1, the regeneration of a brownfield urban area identified (UC1 B) as vacant or derelict in accordance with the character of the community.
- Provision of new housing.
- Consequent provision of affordable housing.
- Provision of local business/employment opportunities.

Evolving national policy

Beyond this, evolving national policy in relation to best practice in architectural design, energy consumption and sustainability provides further contemporary guidance regarding the social, economic and cultural aspirations of wider society.

Regeneration

On the basis that the retention of the listed buildings is not viable and that these cannot be retained, the Developer has instructed the preparation a scheme for the regeneration of the site that:

- is of the highest contemporary architectural and technical quality;

- follows current best practice in relation to the environment and conservation of energy, utilising all of their existing breadth of experience in this
  regard;
- properly meets all of the aspirations for the site set out in the Local Plan;
- properly integrates the site within the context of the wider local
  community.

These proposals are set out in the separate drawings accompanying the
applications for Planning Permission and Listed Building Consent (Figures
2.15 and 2.16).

In this respect the following specific advantages will be derived
from full regeneration of the site:

- The integration of the formerly isolated site into the local urban fabric.
- The avoidance of compensatory 'over development'.
- The development of prototypes for sustainable design.
- The creation of local employment opportunities.
- The creation of meaningful amenity space.
- The creation of affordable housing.

The development appraisal for the proposal indicates a
development yield in the region of 25 per cent, which will provide further
benefits in the form of the level of capital receipt that can be transferred
to the Bearsden Academy PPP.

In terms of the tests set out in SHEP and SPP 23, it can be seen
that the demolition of the remaining residence halls is essential to
delivering the above significant benefits to the wider community.

Conclusion

The Heritage Statement concluded with the justification of why consent for the
demolition of the Listed Buildings should be granted:

Conclusion

The preservation of the Category A Listed Residence Halls at the former
St Andrew's College is not commercially tenable due to the significant level
of on-costs associated with converting the buildings to meet current
building regulations and modern use requirements, coupled with current
and foreseeable market conditions relating to the sale of residential
property. Even taking into account a significant level of 'over-development',
current appraisals show a development loss of over £18.5 million
(equivalent to a negative yield of 31 per cent).

In this regard the regeneration of the eastern part of the original
campus will not be viable if these buildings are to be retained.

2.15
**Submitted indicative
planning proposal
(courtesy of Archial
Architects)**

2.16
**Submitted indicative
planning proposal
(courtesy of Archial
Architects)**

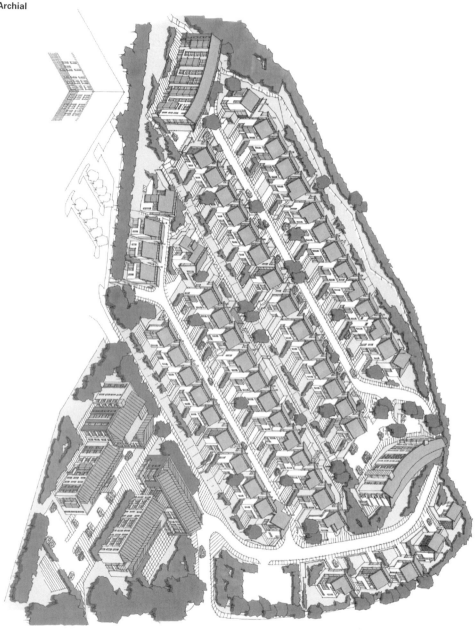

Having been through an extended process of attempting, and being unable, to develop a viable proposal that retains the buildings, the Developer has now submitted applications for Planning and Listed Building Consent for their demolition, under proposals for the complete regeneration of the site.

In this respect it is acknowledged that, whilst there is a requirement to have special regard to the desirability of preserving a listed building, national policy and guidance advise that a case for demolition can be made on the basis that:

- the building is not of special interest; or
- the building is incapable of repair; or
- the demolition of the building is essential to delivering significant benefits to economic growth or the wider community; or
- the repair of the building is not economically viable and that it has been marketed at a price reflecting its location and condition to potential restoring purchasers for a reasonable period.

In these terms the proposed demolition of the Residence Halls can be justified on the basis that their retention is not viable and that their demolition is essential to delivering the significant benefits to the wider community that will be derived from the regeneration of the overall site.

The diminished special interest and present material and structural condition of the listed buildings are mitigating factors.

The specific benefits that will be derived from the regeneration proposals will outweigh the loss of the listed buildings remaining on the eastern part of the former campus site.

The loss of the listed buildings will be regrettable. However, in mitigation there are a number of other extant and more sustainable examples of the work of Gillespie Kidd & Coia from this period.

Executive summary

The application for the regeneration of the site and the potential loss of the Listed Buildings was made in a factionalized political atmosphere. In such a situation, the presentation of the case for consent in a succinct summary became an important consideration:

Executive summary

St Andrew's College, Bearsden (formerly Notre Dame College) became surplus to the University of Glasgow's requirements in 1998 and was vacated in 2002.

Outline Planning Approval was obtained for a mixed-use development incorporating a new secondary school campus and residential and business uses, in 2005. This accepted, in principle, the demolition of the original Administration and Teaching blocks and two, out of five, of the Residential Blocks. The Residential Blocks are Category A Listed.

The Administration and Teaching Blocks have subsequently been demolished, and the new Bearsden Academy is currently being constructed on the western part of the site. The eastern part of the site, which contains the Residential Blocks, remains undeveloped and is in a semi-derelict condition. It is currently under the ownership of East Dunbartonshire Council. This will transfer to Muse Developments during 2009.

This document considers the case for listed building consent for the demolition of the Category A Listed Residence Halls on the basis of the relevant current national and local policy and guidance and concludes the following:

The preservation of the Category A Listed Residence Halls at the former St Andrew's College is not commercially tenable due to the significant level of on-costs associated with converting the buildings to meet current building regulations and modern use requirements coupled with current and foreseeable market conditions relating to the sale of residential property. Even taking into account a significant level of 'over-development', current appraisals show a development loss of over £18.5 million (equivalent to a negative yield of 31 per cent).

In this regard the regeneration of the eastern part of the original campus will not be viable if these buildings are to be retained.

Having been through an extended process of attempting, and being unable, to develop a viable proposal that retains the buildings, the Developer has now submitted applications for Planning and Listed Building consent for their demolition, under proposals for the complete regeneration of the site.

In this respect it is acknowledged that, whilst there is a requirement to have special regard to the desirability of preserving a listed building, national policy and guidance advise that a case for demolition can be made on the basis that:

- the building is not of special interest; or
- the building is incapable of repair; or
- the demolition of the building is essential to delivering significant benefits to economic growth or the wider community; or
- the repair of the building is not economically viable and that it has been marketed at a price reflecting its location and condition to potential restoring purchasers for a reasonable period.

In these terms, the proposed demolition of the Residence Halls can be justified on the basis that their retention is not viable and that their demolition is essential to delivering the significant benefits to the wider community that will be derived from the regeneration of the overall site.

The diminished special interest and present material and structural condition of the listed buildings are mitigating factors.

The specific benefits that will be derived from the regeneration proposals will outweigh the loss of the listed buildings remaining on the eastern part of the former campus site.

The loss of the listed buildings will be regrettable. However, in mitigation, there are a number of other extant and more sustainable examples of the work of Gillespie Kidd & Coia from this period.

Summary

In this instance, the principal case for consent was that the technical problems and costs associated with redeveloping the Listed Buildings made their retention, in any form, unsustainable. This was principally mitigated by the substantial benefits that would be accrued from regenerating the site, clearly correlated to the aspirations expressed within the existing local and regional planning context. The very poor condition of the buildings and the diminished importance of the already partially demolished campus provided further mitigation.

Again, in terms of the Planning (Listed Buildings and Conservation Areas) (Scotland) Act 1997, consideration of the case made within the Heritage Statement was taken to demonstrate that special regard to the desirability of preserving the Listed Buildings and their settings (or any features of special architectural or historic interest which they possessed) was paid on the part of all the relevant decision-making bodies.

Case Study 3

House of Fraser Store, Buchanan Street, Glasgow

Introduction

The wholesale refurbishment of the House of Fraser store in Glasgow commenced with a 'like for like' fit out of the first-floor interiors of the Category A and B Listed Buildings. On the basis of an initial informal discussion with Historic Scotland, the work had proceeded without a formalization of whether or not Listed Building consent was required. Local authority planners visiting the site in relation to the next phase of the work, which involved the fitting out of the interior and replacement of existing shop fronts at ground floor level, raised concerns regarding the impact on the Listed Buildings of the work that had already been undertaken.

I was employed essentially to regularize the planning situation by presenting a formalized Listed Building case.

Again, this is a more recent case utilizing the guidance provided in SHEP and SPP 23 (October 2008). I have incorporated below, more or less, the complete Heritage Statement submitted in support of the applications for Planning and Listed Building consent. Subsequent to the submission, the local authority confirmed that the formal planning situation had now been regularized. Due to changed circumstances at the time of writing the relevant approvals are still awaited.

Introductory section

The introductory sections of the Heritage Statement immediately sought to simplify what had become a relatively emotive planning situation:

Introduction and scope

House of Fraser are preparing to undertake a major refit of their premises in Buchanan Street as part of a long-term commitment to maintaining a high quality department store in the city where they were originally founded.

The works form the current fit out cycle for the store and are in effect a 'like for like' replacement for the outdated 1990s fit out of the previous cycle. In this respect the fitting out at first floor level was completed in September 2008. The Ground Floor works, which include works to the shopfronts facing onto Buchanan Street, are planned to commence in early 2009. The upper floors will be refitted in phases thereafter.

The present store has been formed by the amalgamation of a number of individual retail premises within the Central Conservation Area, incorporating three Listed Buildings (Figures 3.1a–e, 3.2 and 3.3a–d):

134–156 Argyle Street and 3–7 Buchanan Street	Category B Listed	Figs 3.1b, c & 3.3b
21–31 Buchanan Street	Category A Listed	Figs 3.1d & 3.3c
45 Buchanan Street	Category A Listed	Figs 3.1e & 3.3d

3.1a
Elevations of existing buildings (courtesy of Hurd Rolland Partnership/ Havelock Europa)

Glasgow City Council has advised that Listed Building Consent is required for the works.

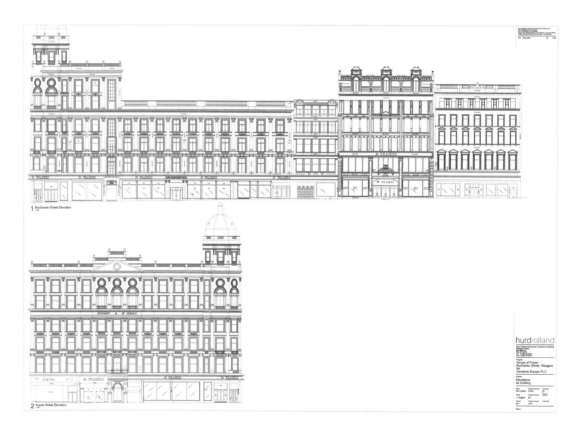

3.1b
**134–156 Argyle
Street (existing)
(courtesy of Hurd
Rolland Partnership/
Havelock Europa)**

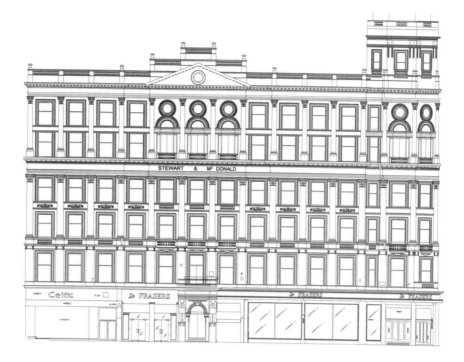

3.1c
**3–7 Buchanan Street (existing) (courtesy
of Hurd Rolland Partnership/Havelock
Europa)**

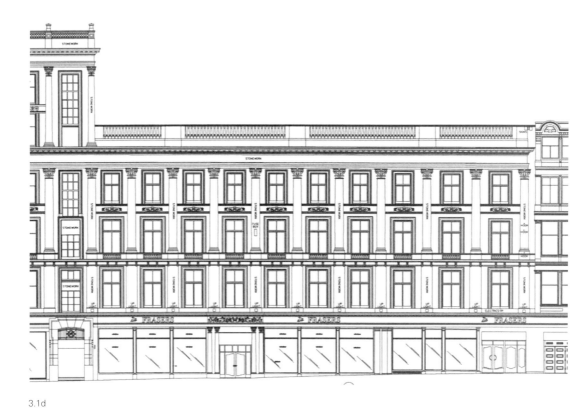

3.1d
21–31 Buchanan Street (existing) (courtesy of Hurd Rolland Partnership/Havelock Europa)

3.1e
45 Buchanan Street (existing) (courtesy of Hurd Rolland Partnership/Havelock Europa)

3.2
Listed Buildings ©
Crown Copyright
and/or database
right. All rights
reserved. Licence
number 100049743

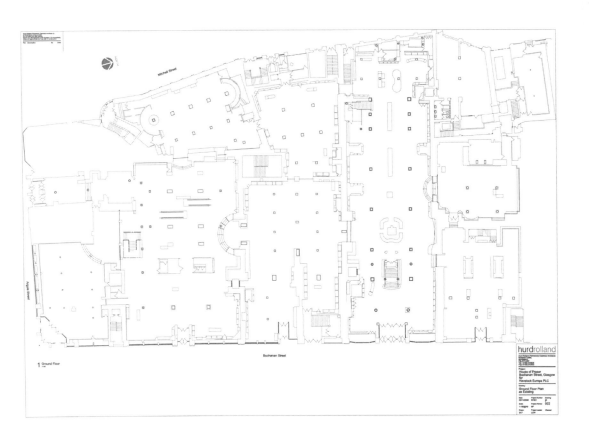

3.3a
Existing ground floor plan (courtesy of Hurd Rolland Partnership/Havelock Europa)

3.3b
**134–156 Argyle Street, 3–7 Buchanan Street
(existing) (courtesy of Hurd Rolland
Partnership/Havelock Europa)**

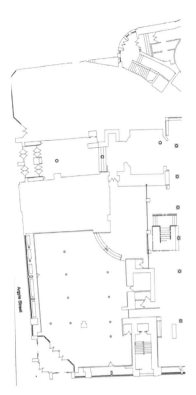

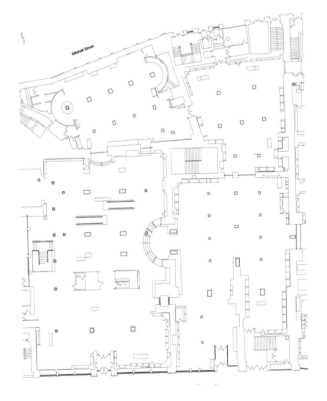

3.3c
**21–31 Buchanan Street,
8–20 Mitchell Street
(existing) (courtesy of
Hurd Rolland Partnership/
Havelock Europa)**

3.3d
**45 Buchanan Street,
34–50 Mitchell Street
(existing) (courtesy
of Hurd Rolland
Partnership/
Havelock Europa)**

The Hurd Rolland Partnership has been appointed by House of Fraser to assess the extent, if any, that the proposed works will affect the special interest of the listed buildings and, if necessary, to prepare a case for listed building consent in terms of current national policy and guidance . . .

Drawings and specifications have been submitted in support of separate applications for Planning and Listed Building Consent for the works at ground and first floor level.

This document provides an assessment of the impact that these works will have on the special interest of the various listed buildings that comprise the store and where appropriate provides justification for the works in terms of current national policy and guidance.

In this respect the baseline condition has been taken to be the present store configuration or, in the case of the first floor, the configuration that existed prior to the commencement of the recently completed work.

The Glasgow City Plan incorporates design policy in relation to shop fronts, signage and other relevant issues. These matters fall outwith the scope of this document but will be material considerations in relation to approving Planning Consent.

Policy and guidance

The following section set out the central relevant policy and guidance that formed the basis of the case for consent:

Policy and guidance

Relevant current policy and guidance includes:

- SPP 23: Planning and Historic Environment.
- Scottish Historic Environment Policy (SHEP).
- The Memorandum of Guidance on Listed Buildings and Conservation Areas (1998).
- The Glasgow City Plan.

SPP 23: Planning and Historic Environment

SPP 23: Planning and Historic Environment superseded NPPG 18: Planning and the Historic Environment and NPPG 5: Archaeology and Planning in October 2008. It sets out the national planning policy for the historic environment and indicates how the planning system will contribute towards the delivery of Scottish Ministers' policies as set out in SHEP.

Scottish Historic Environment Policy (SHEP)

The SHEP series of consultative policy documents was originally developed as a response to the review of Historic Scotland in 2003/2004. The Scottish Historic Environment Policy (SHEP), published by Historic Scotland in October 2008, consolidated these documents into a single comprehensive policy document setting out the Scottish Ministers' policies for the historic environment with the stated aim of providing greater policy direction for Historic Scotland and a framework to inform the day-to-day work of a range of organisations that have a role and interest in managing the historic environment. SHEP formally supersedes the policy elements of the Memorandum of Guidance on Listed Buildings and Conservation Areas (the remaining technical annexes to the Memorandum will be withdrawn in Spring 2009).

Memorandum for Guidance on Listed Buildings and Conservation Areas

The Memorandum for Guidance on Listed Buildings and Conservation Areas (revised 1998), published by Historic Scotland, was formerly recognised as the primary source of guidance regarding the Scottish Ministers' interests and responsibilities in relation to Listed Buildings and Conservation Areas. It is being withdrawn in stages between March 2008 and March 2009. Sections on policy were replaced by SHEP in October 2008. The technical annexes will, in due course, be replaced by a suite of guidance papers.

Glasgow City Plan

The Glasgow City Plan was adopted in August 2003. A finalised draft of City Plan 2, setting out emerging local policy, was published in May 2007.

Conservation policy contained within the City Plan is generally consistent with national policy.

Historical background

The Statement continued with an analysis of the evolution of the buildings comprising the present-day store, based on OS map and historic photographic evidence:

Historical background

Introduction

The original store, owned by Hugh Fraser, consisted of a small drapers shop at the corner of Argyle Street and Buchanan Street, opened in 1849 (Figure 3.4).

The present House of Fraser store on Buchanan Street extends to Argyle Street at ground floor level and throughout the full height of conjoined accommodation at 21–45 Buchanan Street and 8–50 Mitchell Street (Figures 3.1 and 3.3).

This section provides a brief history of the individual buildings that make up the present day store.

21–31 Buchanan Street and 8–20 Mitchell Street

The premises at 21–31 Buchanan Street were created in 1879 by merging a conglomeration of existing buildings and sites between Buchanan Street and Mitchell Street into one large block. Unifying façades were applied to both frontages, a classically ordered ashlar stone façade at the principal elevation overlooking Buchanan Street and a more utilitarian façade at the rear elevation facing into Mitchell Street (Figures 3.1d and 3.5). Though not expressed externally, the walls of the retained buildings became sub-stantial sub-divisional elements within the interior of the new premises, slapped through to provide internal connections as necessary (Figure 3.3b).

45 Buchanan Street and 34–50 Mitchell Street

The building presently described as 45 Buchanan Street originally con-sisted of three separate warehouse buildings facing onto Buchanan Street (five when the original buildings at 42–50 Mitchell Street, at the rear of the northernmost warehouse, are taken into account). A substantial fire in 1883 destroyed the original central building of the three.

3.4

Close-up from 1856 OS map. Reproduced by permission of the Trustees of the National Library of Scotland

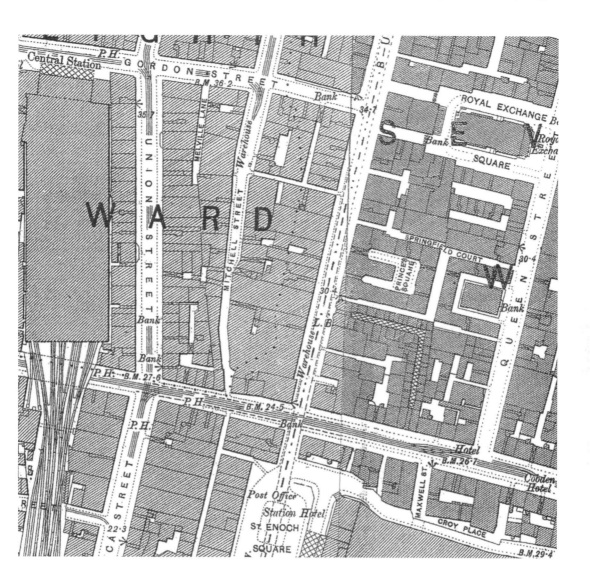

3.5
**Close-up from 1896
OS map. Reproduced
by permission of the
Trustees of the
National Library of
Scotland**

The narrow southernmost building was originally erected in 1854 (Figure 3.4) but from photographic evidence appears to have been substantially rebuilt subsequent to the fire in 1883. At the very least, two additional floors and the cast iron façade fronting onto Buchanan Street appear to have been added at this time (Figure 3.1e).

The Wylie & Lochhead building, the central building of the three, was erected in 1884 replacing the destroyed warehouse that previously extended from Buchanan Street to Mitchell Street (Figures 3.1e, 3.5–3.7). The new building was of an ostentatious baroque renaissance style accommodating, on its central east/west axis, the five-storey gallery that is the main internal feature of the present store. It provided the most ornate of the three façades facing onto Buchanan Street.

The northernmost building on Buchanan Street predated the fire but two storeys were added almost immediately thereafter (Figures 3.1e, 3.4, 3.5, 3.8 and 3.9). The two utilitarian buildings to the rear, facing onto Mitchell Street, appear to have been unaffected by the fire and remained separate up until the late 1930s.

The three previously separate buildings (along with the buildings on Mitchell Street) were, around 1938, merged into a single large store similar in size to that at 21–31 Buchanan Street (Figures 3.1e and 3.3d). Like 21–31 Buchanan Street, the party walls became dominant sub-divisional elements within the internal layout of the new store, with structural slappings created as and where necessary to provide through flow (Figure 3.3d).

In an attempt to create the sense of a unified store, a modern ground floor shop frontage and canopy were extended across the front of the combined Buchanan Street properties in 1938 (Figures 3.8, 3.11 and 3.12).

134–156 Argyle Street and 3–7 Buchanan Street

House of Fraser only occupy part of the ground floor of the building at 134–156 Argyle Street and 3–7 Buchanan Street (Figure 3.3b).

The building was erected in 1903 and above street level is a carefully ordered homogenous classically styled edifice (Figures 3.1b and c). At street level the building was always designed to accommodate separate retail units (Figures 3.10, 3.13 and 3.14).

Present

Elements of the ground floor of 134–156 Argyle Street and 3–7 Buchanan Street and the whole of the buildings at 21–31 and 45 Buchanan Street were conjoined during the 1980s and have existed in this configuration as a large department store since then (Figures 3.3a–d). The presently existing elevations are shown on drawings submitted with the applications for planning and Listed Building consent (Figures 3.1a–e).

At 134–156 Argyle Street and 3–7 Buchanan Street the present shop fronts are of a utilitarian modern design. The entrance into House of Fraser at 152 Argyle Street has applied pilasters and a deepened dado concealing a dropped suspended ceiling beyond (Figure 3.1b).

The shop front at 134–140 Argyle Street and 1–5 Buchanan Street was installed in the 1990s and was part of an attempt to unify the appearance of the various premises that had been merged by House of Fraser (Figures 3.1b, c, 3.14 and 3.15). It replaced a previous rag tag of utilitarian shop fronts (Figures 3.13 and 3.16). The cornice and dado appear to have been stripped back to the original at that time. A blind box and the egg and dart mouldings beneath the cornice are additions (Figures 3.14 and 3.15).

45 Buchanan Street,
middle section, 1937.
Glasgow City
Archives and Special
Collections, The
Mitchell Library,
Culture and Sport
Glasgow

3.7
45 Buchanan Street,
middle section, 2008
(courtesy of Hurd
Rolland Partnership)

3.8
45 Buchanan Street, north section,
1938. Glasgow City Archives and
Special Collections, The Mitchell
Library, Culture and Sport Glasgow

3.9
45 Buchanan Street,
north section, 2008
(courtesy of Hurd
Rolland Partnership)

3.10
**Close-up from 1913 OS map.
Reproduced by permission of the
Trustees of the National Library
of Scotland**

3.11
**Close-up from 1934 OS map.
Reproduced by permission of the
Trustees of the National Library of
Scotland**

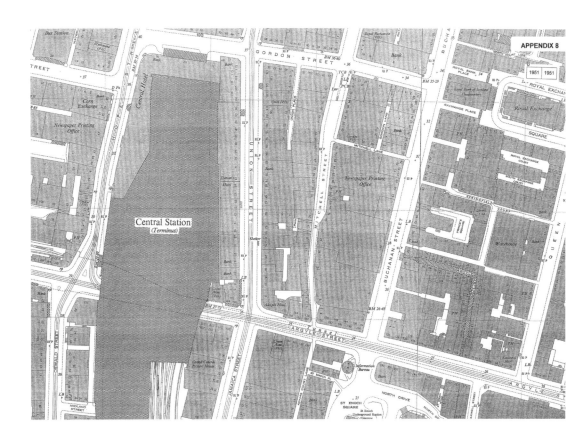

3.12
**Extract from 1951
OS map. Reproduced
by permission of
the Trustees of the
National Library of
Scotland**

3.13
**1–3 Buchanan Street,
1938. Glasgow City
Archives and Special
Collections, The
Mitchell Library,
Culture and Sport
Glasgow**

3.14
1–3 Buchanan Street, 2008 (courtesy of Hurd Rolland Partnership/ Havelock Europa)

The champfered corner arrangement was initially created in the 1930s (Figure 3.13). The 1990s' refit attempted, unsuccessfully, to minimise the impact of the corner column [Figure 3.14].

The doorway at No. 7 Buchanan Street is Art Deco in appearance and was in all likelihood applied in the late 1920s/early 1930s (Figures 3.15 and 3.16).

The shop front from beyond No. 7 Buchanan Street up to the former Wylie & Lochhead building was part of the 1990s' attempt to unify the House of Fraser frontage (Figures 3.1d and e). In this instance the original subdividing columns have been retained, but new screens have been installed and the blind boxes continued across the foot of the dado. The egg and dart motif is authentic across 21–31 Buchanan Street but is applied at the southern part of 45, where the canopy was removed when 21–31 and 45 Buchanan Street were merged.

As part of the 1990s' works, subsequent to the removal of the canopy combining the three separate frontages at 45 Buchanan Street, an attempt was made to re-establish the earlier elegance of the Wylie & Lochhead entrance façade. Where the terracotta column cladding had

3.15
7 Buchanan Street, 2008 (courtesy of Hurd
Rolland Partnership/Havelock Europa)

3.16
5–7 Buchanan Street,
1938. Glasgow City
Archives and Special
Collections, The
Mitchell Library,
Culture and Sport
Glasgow

previously been removed, a mock terracotta casing (moulded in glass reinforced plastic (GRP)) was reintroduced. Similarly the flat arch located over the entrance doors, also constructed from GRP, was also introduced at that time (Figures 3.6 and 3.7). All of the GRP elements have subsequently been painted. The column bases at either side of the entrance doors are clad in sandstone. Again these are not original.

The doors and shop screens are not original (Figure 3.7).

The attempt to unify the store façades to the south of the Wylie & Lochhead frontage was continued across the shop fronts at the northern part of 45 Buchanan Street. In this instance, an entirely new cornice and dado were clumsily applied, along with blind boxes, across the whole frontage (Figures 3.8 and 3.9). Again the store screens are not original.

The present 1990s' interiors were designed to create a generally consistent level of contemporary appearance throughout the merged buildings. In this respect the many incongruous interfaces between the various building elements that comprise the store were generally concealed behind modern wall panels, suspended ceilings and column casings in a similar manner to which the interiors of the various earlier configurations of merged buildings will have been fitted out.

Within the expanded shop unit accessed from the corner of Argyle Street and Buchanan Street, the original columns and ceilings were generally left exposed alongside contemporary services and lighting for stylistic reasons.

Within the interior of the former Wylie & Lochhead part of the store, the original architectural features were deliberately exposed and integrated within the interior design.

Proposed fit out

The proposed fitting out and shop front works are the next in the cycle of works that have historically maintained these buildings in department store use either individually or in combination.

Assessment of proposals on the basis of the key policy and guidance

Thereafter, the Heritage Statement provided an assessment of the proposed refurbishment in terms of the relevant key policy and guidance:

Key policy and guidance

Introduction

The upgrading of shops, offices and other such uses, that are reliant upon high quality contemporary appearance as an essential part of their business, is a key economic driver for maintaining and enhancing the historic environment.

In this respect refitting and upgrading work is a cyclical process that affects the vast majority of listed office buildings, hotels and department stores in city centres throughout the United Kingdom. Whilst such works can involve the dismantling and replacement of superficial elements such as suspended ceilings and fixed shelving and furnishing, more often than not, they can have a low level of impact upon the special architectural or historic interest of the buildings within which they are carried out, and in many cases listed building consent is not required.

Within this section reference is made to key national policy and guidance relevant to the proposed works at House of Fraser.

Planning (Listed Buildings and Conservation Areas) (Scotland) Act 1997

The statutory requirement regarding work affecting listed buildings is stated in the Planning (Listed Buildings and Conservation Areas) (Scotland) Act 1997:

General duty as respects listed buildings in exercise of planning functions

59(1) In considering whether to grant planning permission for development which affects a listed building or its setting, a planning authority or the Secretary of State [the Scottish Ministers], as the case may be, shall have special regard to the desirability of preserving the building or its setting or any features of special architectural or historic interest which it possesses.

Decision on application

14(2) In considering whether to grant listed building consent for any works, the planning authority or the Secretary of State [the Scottish Ministers], as the case may be, shall have special regard to the desirability of preserving the building or its setting or any features of special architectural or historic interest which it possesses.

SPP 23: Planning and historic environment

Under the heading 'Sustainable development and the historic environment', SPP 23 states:

4. The historic environment can play a key part in promoting sustainable economic growth and regeneration by offering attractive living and working conditions that will encourage inward investment. It is of particular importance for supporting the sustainable growth of tourism and leisure.

In relation to Listed Buildings, SPP 23 states:

13. Listed buildings are buildings of special architectural or historic interest and are listed by Historic Scotland on behalf of Scottish Ministers . . . Listing covers the whole of a building including its interior and any ancillary structures within its curtilage provided these were constructed before 1 July 1948. Change should be managed to protect a building's special interest while enabling it to remain in active use . . .

35. Once a building is listed, any . . . works which alter or extend the building in a way which would affect its character or its setting as a building of special architectural or historic interest, require listed building consent. It is for the planning authority to . . . consider whether the proposed works will require listed building consent . . .

36. Scottish Ministers' policies on listed building consent and on the considerations to be taken account by planning authorities in determining listed building consent applications for alteration, adaptation or demolition of a listed building are set out in the current SHEP.

Regarding 'Conservation Areas', SPP 23 notes:

14. Conservation Areas are areas of special architectural or historic interest, the character or appearance of which it is desirable to preserve or enhance . . .

Scottish Historic Environment Policy (SHEP)

The general policy chapter of SHEP states:

1.6 . . . The challenge for sustainable management of the historic environment and how it contributes to the vitality of modern life, is to identify its key characteristics and to establish the boundaries within which change can continue so that it enhances rather than diminishes historic character.

1.8 *The protection of the historic environment is not about preventing change*. Ministers believe that change in this dynamic environment should be *managed intelligently and with understanding*, to achieve the best outcome for the historic environment and for the people of Scotland. Such decisions often have to recognise economic realities.

Under the heading 'Key principles', Chapter 1 states:

1.15 The conservation of any part of Scotland's historic environment should . . . ensure that, where change is proposed, it is appropriate, carefully considered, authoritatively based, properly planned and executed, and (if appropriate) reversible.

Chapter 1 continues, under the heading 'Investment in the historic environment':

1.44 Scottish Ministers recognise that investment in the fabric and management of Scotland's historic environment is needed to meet the objectives they have set for its care, protection and enhancement, and for increasing public appreciation and enjoyment. Investment will also ensure that the historic environment is maintained as an irreplaceable asset that makes a major contribution to Scotland's economic, social and cultural well-being. Ministers are committed to promoting high-quality standards of repair, maintenance, and conservation and the sympathetic re-use of heritage assets where this is appropriate.

Within Chapter 3, regarding Listed Building consent, SHEP states:

3.32 Listed buildings are protected under the Planning (Listed Buildings and Conservation Areas) (Scotland) Act 1997. This establishes that any work which affects the character of a listed building will require listed building consent . . .

3.33 In assessing an application for listed building consent, the planning authority is required to have special regard to the desirability of preserving the building, or its setting, or any features of special architectural or historic interest which it possesses.

3.34 Works of like-for-like repair or other works which do not affect a building's character, would not normally require listed building consent. Such works could include . . . altering part of a building which does not contribute to the overall special interest.

In Chapter 3, under the heading 'Scottish Minister's policy on Listed Building consent', SHEP continues:

3.40 Scottish Ministers are committed to the sustainable use and management of the historic environment. This means meeting the needs of today without compromising the opportunity for future generations to understand, appreciate and benefit from the historic environment.

3.42 Once lost listed buildings cannot be replaced. They can be robbed of their special interest either by inappropriate alteration or by demolition. There is, therefore, a presumption against demolition or other works that adversely affect the special interest of a listed building or its setting.

3.43 Listed buildings will however, like other buildings, require alteration and adaptation from time to time if they are to remain in beneficial use, and will be at risk if such alteration and adaptation is unduly constrained. In most cases such change, if approached carefully, can be managed without adversely affecting the special interest of the building.

Regarding determination, SHEP states:

3.50 Where a proposal involves alteration or adaptation which will sustain or enhance the beneficial use of the building and does not adversely affect the special interest of the building, consent should normally be granted.

3.51 Where a proposal involves alteration or adaptation which will have an adverse or significantly adverse impact on the special interest of the building, planning authorities, in reaching decisions should consider carefully:

a. the relative importance of the special interest of the building; and

b. the scale of the impact of the proposals on that special interest; and

c. whether there are other options which would ensure a continuing beneficial use for the building with less impact on its special interest; and

d. whether there are significant benefits for economic growth or the wider community which justify a departure from the presumption set out in paragraph 3.42 above.

This Section concluded:

Summary

It can be seen that current national policy and guidance recognise that change that will maintain and enhance what is important within the historic environment can provide wider social and economic benefits to the local community. Key to this is that the special interest of listed buildings and other heritage designations are identified at the outset and that change is managed accordingly.

In relation to the proposed upgrading works at House of Fraser key factors are:

• the assessment of what is of special architectural or historic interest;
• the specific scale of any impact on this special interest set against any social, economic and cultural benefits to the wider community;
• where appropriate the reversibility of the works.

Special interest

The Heritage Statement continued with the assessment of the special interest of the Listed Buildings in terms of the guidance set out in SHEP.

Introduction

Within this section an assessment of the special architectural and historic interest of each of the listed buildings that comprise the present House of Fraser Store is made in terms of current national policy and guidance.
The store comprises the following Listed Buildings:

134–156 Argyle Street and 3–7 Buchanan Street	Category B Listed	Figs 3.1b, c & 3.3b
21–31 Buchanan Street	Category A Listed	Figs 3.1d & 3.3c
45 Buchanan Street	Category A Listed	Figs 3.1e & 3.3d

Category of Listing

Regarding the categories of listing, Note 2.19 of SHEP states:

> Listed buildings are given categories of listing which distinguish their relative merit. These categories have no statutory weight but are advisory. They inform levels of designation and grant award. There are three categories, defined as follows:
>
> A: buildings of national or international importance, either architectural or historic, or fine little-altered examples of some particular period style or building type;
>
> B: buildings of regional or more than local importance, or major examples of some particular period, style or building type . . .

Criteria and principles of Listing

Annexe 2 to SHEP sets out the criteria for determining whether a building is of 'special architectural or historic interest':

1. The criteria can only provide a framework within which professional judgement is exercised in reaching individual decisions.
2. To be listed, a building need not be functioning for the purpose originally intended. For example, a redundant railway viaduct may have continued its life as a walkway or cycle path, even a wildlife sanctuary.
3. The principles of selection for statutory listing are broadly:
   a. age and rarity;
   b. architectural or historic interest;
   c. close historical associations.

Architectural or historic interest

Regarding architectural or historic interest Annexe 2 states:

> 9. Selection for architectural or historic interest is assessed under a range of broad headings, summarised below.

10. Interior: Interior design and fixed decorative schemes of … business premises in all their variation can add to the case for listing. Examples include skirting boards, plasterwork, dado rails, chimney-pieces, staircases, doors and over-door panels, ornate radiators, floor grilles, sanitary ware, the existence of box-beds, vaulted basement or wine cellar divisions, slate shelving, servant bell systems, shop or pub fittings and fixed internal machinery.

11. Plan Form: The internal planning of buildings is instructive and can be ingenious although it may not be evident on the exterior …

12. Technological excellence or innovation, material or design quality: Evidence of structural or material innovation adds weight to a decision. Exceptional structural form can be significant and is found across the wide variety of building types from a cruck-framed barn to an early iron-framed jute mill or steel-framed office block. Exceptional use of materials or use of fine material may be a factor. Style will be considered against relevant conventions particularly for its quality or exceptional interest.

134–156 Argyle Street and 3–7 Buchanan Street

The Information Supplementary to the Statutory List, produced by Historic Scotland, provides the following description in relation to 134–156 Argyle Street and 3–7 Buchanan Street:

Horatio K. Bromhead, completed 1903. Free classical warehouse. 6-storeys and canted angle turret. Modern shops at ground. 13 × 5 bays and single corner bay. Polished ashlar. Sash and case windows, some altered to T-pane casements on cill band, graduated recessed architraves. Giant order of Corinthian pilasters and semi-engaged columns rising from 1st to 2nd floors and repeated above at 3rd and 4th floors, sculpted panels between floors. Modillion cornice at 3rd and 5th floors; continuous balustrade with panelled, corniced piers. Corner section: canted bays, balcony at 1st floor, independent circular balconies at 2nd stylised Venetian windows with oculi above at 4th and 5th floors; polygonal turret with balconies, consoled cornice, balustrade, columned roof lantern.

ELEVATION TO ARGYLE STREET: bays arranged 3–1–3–1–3, 3-bay sections breaking forward; central doorway with stooping Atlantes carrying curving 1st floor balcony; independent balconies in 3-bay section of 2nd floor above; pedimented with stepped balustrade and Venetians as corner section at 4th and 5th floors.

ELEVATION TO BUCHANAN STREET: N 3-bay section as outer bays to Argyle Street.

Assessment

The special interest of this building relates to its exterior architectural quality, specifically from first floor level upwards, at Argyle Street and Buchanan Street (Figures 3.1b and c).

House of Fraser only occupies the ground floor units at the corner of Argyle Street/Buchanan Street and a central unit of this building. In this respect the shop units at ground floor level have been inter-changeable elements since the building was originally erected, and it is the continual upgrading of these shop fronts that is of relevant importance (Figures 3.13, 3.14 and 3.16).

Remaining original interior features are of some architectural interest and are presently exposed for stylistic reasons. Instances of irregular column spacing reflect the utiltarian alterations and removals of load-bearing sub-dividing walls that have taken place during the life of the building. Where they are visible, original internal features generally bear little relationship to the present internal plan configuration [Figure 3.3b].

It should be noted that the fitting-out works proposed by House of Fraser in this area will have no physical impact on any remaining internal features. The original architectural features will be less exposed than in the previous fit out, in line with the new higher-quality commercial use of this area.

21–31 Buchanan Street

The supplementary information provided by Historic Scotland in relation to 21–31 Buchanan Street and 8–28 Mitchell Street states:

> William Spence, circa 1879. 4-storey, 10-bay warehouse/department store with classical details. Modern ground floor, shop front. Painted ashlar façade, cast-iron frame. Coupled Corinthian pilastered doorpiece with sculpted frieze. 1st floor plain pilasters. Giant order of Corinthian pilasters rising from 2nd to 3rd floor; blind balustrade to 2nd floor windows. Sculpted details between 2nd and 3rd floors. Entablature and main cornice. Balustraded parapet. Corinthian columned interior.

Assessment

Again, the special interest of the building relates to its external architectural quality. In this instance, particularly the classically ordered façade overlooking Buchanan Street, that was applied to the new and retained interior elements that comprised the building's original interior (Figures 3.1d and 3.3c). In this respect the unifying façade onto Mitchell Street is also of some architectural interest.

Similar to 134–156 Argyle Street and 3–7 Buchanan Street, the shop fronts at Buchanan Street have been changed over the years to address contemporary tastes, although the original columns have remained exposed over the period.

The interior of the building consists of a relatively regular central portion accessed directly from Buchanan Street; this is bounded to the north and west by the external walls of two retained earlier buildings. The area to the rear of the store (adjacent Mitchell Street) is an almost self-contained element accessed through openings slapped in the previously external sub-dividing wall. To its immediate north it feeds into a utilitarian infill area, created at the same time as the main central space, through a further slapped opening (Figure 3.3c).

Similarly, the earlier building to the north of the main floor space is still evident. However, in this instance, the party wall that previously subdivided 33 from 45 Buchanan Street has been substantially removed (Figure 3.3c).

Taken as a whole, the internal column arrangements reflect that, when created, 21–31 Buchanan Street retained large elements of earlier buildings. This is further complicated by additional columns that have been inserted during subsequent alterations that have been under-taken to create additional access as and where necessary (Figure 3.3c).

Similar to 134–156 Argyle Street and 3–7 Buchanan Street, any remaining original interior features have little significant architectural quality in their own right. Rather, they hold lesser interest as a record of the previous configurations of the various buildings that were brought together behind the unifying façades. In this case, they are all generally concealed behind modern suspended ceilings, column casings and wall claddings.

Again, the fitting out works proposed by House of Fraser in this area will have no physical impact on any remaining internal features. Rather, these will generally remain concealed and be retained in their present condition.

45 Buchanan Street and 34–50 Mitchell Street

The supplementary information provided by Historic Scotland in relation to 45 Buchanan Street and 34–50 Mitchell Street states:

> 3 separate warehouse premises now combined into one depart-ment store.
>
> S section of Buchanan Street frontage (originally Kemp's shawl emporium) 1853–4, 5 storeys (4th and 5th added by Boucher and Cousland after fire of 1883). Cast-iron framed, pilastered masonry ends, diminutive segmental pediments over end bays.
>
> Central section (original Wylie and Lochhead building). James Sellars (Campbell Douglas and Sellars) 1884 (rebuilt after

fire of 1883). Renaissance 5-storey and attic terracotta frontage, Corinthian pilasters through lower 2 floors, central broken segmental pediment with figures over entrance; divided into 3 bays above ground floor with banded pilasters, 3 windows to each bay, pilastered to 2nd and columned to 3rd; windows in outer bays, bowed at 2nd and 3rd floors; decorated pilasters to 3rd. Balustraded parapet with 3 tall arched dormers, whole surmounted by cast-iron parapet.

INTERIOR: cast-iron framed, clad in terracotta, fireproof construction. Long saloon rising 5 storeys, 4 main bays, arched glass roof, mahogany staircase.

N SECTION: Boucher and Cousland for Mirrlees, Italianate astylar, 5-storey, 7-bay. Top 2 storeys after 1883 fire. Consoled pediments 1st floor windows, segmental pediments 2nd, architraves 3rd, plain pilasters between 4th; balustraded parapet with coat of arms.

Assessment

The special interest of the northern and the southern elements of 45 Buchanan Street again relates to the architectural quality of the external façades facing onto Buchanan Street (Figure 3.1e). Again, the shop fronts at street level have been subject to the vagaries of contemporary styling over the years, most notably when the three separate buildings were merged in 1938 (Figures 3.7 and 3.9).

Similar to the buildings discussed above, the internal arrangements and original architectural features at the interior of these flanking elements are of little inherent architectural quality and, in any event, will not be physically impacted upon by the proposed works.

The central part of 45 Buchanan Street consists of the entirely new building constructed for Wylie & Lochhead on the site cleared after the fire of 1883 (Figures 3.1e, 3.7 and 3.3d). In this respect it is the single element of the many elements that comprise the present House of Fraser store that has an architectural integrity that extends throughout both the exterior and interior of the building.

The key elements of special interest for this part of the building relate to the ornate façade facing onto Buchanan Street, the axial progression of interior spaces, the mahogany main staircase and central gallery, the rear storage area, and ultimately the façade facing onto Mitchell Street.

In this respect any retained interior features more properly relate to an original building configuration and are of a higher value than elsewhere in the store.

It should be noted that not even this grand edifice escaped the attempt to unify the shop frontage onto Buchanan Street when the buildings were merged in 1938. It was only in the 1990s that a not entirely successful attempt was made to restore some of the original quality at street level (Figure 3.7).

Again, the fitting out works proposed by House of Fraser will have no physical impact on remaining internal architectural features. However, in this part of the store, the higher interior quality of the original building provides more opportunity to meaningfully enhance original architectural features.

Summary

With the exception of the former Wylie & Lochhead building, the special architectural interest of the listed buildings that comprise the present-day House of Fraser Store essentially relates to their individual façades, generally from first floor level upwards facing out onto Buchanan Street and Argyle Street (and in some cases onto Mitchell Street).

In relation to the former Wylie & Lochhead building, the special architectural interest extends to the façades on both Buchanan Street and Mitchell Street and to the original interior architectural features of the building, most importantly the mahogany staircase, the five-storey gallery and the glass roof over. In this respect presently concealed architectural features are likely to be of some interest.

The sub-divisional elements and original architectural features within the other areas of the store have some importance as a record of the store's evolution from the various essentially utilitarian building forms that predated the merging of the buildings at 21–31 and 45 Buchanan Street.

The following section of this document considers the impact that the proposed fitting out and shop front works will have on this special interest.

Scale of impact

Thereafter, an assessment of the impact that the proposed refurbishment would have on the Listed Buildings was provided:

Introduction

The proposed works (and in the case of the first floor works, completed works) generally comprise a high-quality upgrading and/or replacement of the presently existing fit out and shop fronts to meet with contemporary retail requirements and expectations and include:

- Reinstatement of the previously existing access stair between ground and first floors.

- Reconfiguration of the existing access stair between ground floor and basement.
- Formation of new staff stair to link the ground floor to the existing staff stair.
- Formation of a new platform lift to provide disabled access to the restaurant.
- Internal refitting of shopfittings; adjustment to ceilings, lighting and services; new floor coverings.
- Reconfiguration of entrance and installation of new shopfronts on corner of Argyle Street/Buchanan Street.
- Replacement of existing entrances with new glass doors and black tiled surrounds.
- Replacement of existing shop windows with new single-pane windows in black aluminium frames.
- Provision of new fascia/signage in black stove enamelled aluminium with illuminated lettering.
- Install flags/banners in existing sockets.

The full scope of works is set out on the drawings submitted for Listed Building and Planning consent. The impact of these works on the special interest of the listed buildings is considered below:

Reinstatement of the previously existing access stair between ground and first floors

As part of the first floor works a new stair has been installed within the rear part of 21–31 Buchanan Street and 8–28 Mitchell Street (Figure 3.18). It is understood that, during the previous fit out, an earlier (but not necessarily original) stair had been removed from this location.

The stair has been installed to improve access within the building at this location and consequently is of practical benefit to users of the store. It is constructed from high-quality materials and is of contemporary design.

The stair has been located within an existing light well that may or may not date back to the original building but certainly has been in existence over a number of refit cycles. It is a natural and appropriate location for an access stair

Whilst the light well is an interesting architectural feature at this particular location, it is not a feature of special interest that has resulted in the building being listed.

In terms of the relevant guidance, it is considered that the insertion of the new stair has had no impact upon the special interest of the listed building and will be highly beneficial to continuing its historic use as a department store.

In common with all of the works to be undertaken during the present refit cycle, these works are reversible.

Reconfiguration of the existing access stair between ground floor and basement

It is proposed to reduce the footprint of the existing stair between ground floor level and basement level at 21–31 Buchanan Street, which presently encroaches on the through flow of space between the retail accommodation in 3–7 Buchanan and 21–31 Buchanan Street (Figure 3.18). This will beneficially reduce visual clutter at this location and improve access through the store both of which will benefit.

The reconfigured stair will be of a high-quality contemporary appearance and generally less visually obtrusive than the present configuration.

The existing stair is not original and is essentially of a functional nature. It is an example of the utilitarian alterations to the building that have occurred throughout its history as an essential part of its ongoing practical use. It is not a feature of special interest that has resulted in the building being listed.

In this respect in terms of the relevant guidance, the reconfiguration of the existing stair will have no impact upon the special interest of the listed building and, again, will be highly beneficial to continuing its historic use as a department store.

Formation of new staff stair to link the ground floor to the existing staff stair

It is proposed to create a new access into the existing staff stair located within an existing stairwell to the rear of 21–31 Buchanan Street. The existing stairwell is not original but dates back to the early reconfigurations of the building that took place at the beginning of the twentieth century (Figure 3.18).

The proposed works will involve breaking into the stairwell and through the ground floor and the creation of an understated enclosure within the main room. The proposal is of a functional nature similar to many such minor insertions made to improve access through the buildings over the period that they have been used as a department store.

The existing stairwell was a functional addition. It is not specifically a feature of special architectural or historic interest. Rather, it is an element that can be seen as part of the record of utilitarian change to the building over its lifetime. Similarly, any skirting or cornicing at basement level, if installed at all, will be of a utilitarian nature. This will be confirmed prior to the commencement of the works.

In terms of the relevant guidance, it is considered that the creation of this new access will have no impact upon the special interest of the listed building and will be beneficial to continuing its historic use as a department store.

Again, the work is essentially reversible.

Formation of a new platform lift to provide disabled access to the restaurant

The installation of a platform lift is required to provide disabled access to the restaurant in northern section of 45 Buchanan Street. It is proposed to create a new slapping that will essentially mirror a previously created opening at the other side of the stairwell at the rear wall of this part of the store (Figure 3.18).

The presence of any significant skirtings will be confirmed prior to the commencement of the works.

In real terms the work is of a functional nature consistent with how the building has been developed throughout its history as a department store.

In terms of the relevant guidance, it is considered that the installation of the new platform lift will have no impact upon the special interest of the listed building and will be highly beneficial to disabled users of the store. The work is essentially reversible.

Internal refitting of shopfittings; adjustment to ceilings, lighting and services; new floor coverings

The internal refit will be a high-quality, 'like for like' upgrade of the existing fit out to meet with contemporary retail requirements and expectations. It comprises the key element of the proposed works and by its very nature is designed to enhance the present use of the store over the next five to ten years.

Key components of the refit will be the replacement of wall claddings, suspended ceilings, lighting and services, column casings, floor coverings and new portals at existing openings between the various building elements that comprise the store. These works will generally be restricted to the existing store areas out with the former Wylie & Lochhead part of the store, which, with the exception of the installation of new entrance portals and upgraded lighting and services, will essentially only be redecorated.

The works at first floor level are already completed.

It should be recognised that existing services runs and ducting are presently concealed behind the existing fit out. It is proposed that, where appropriate, redundant services are stripped out; however, as is normal in such work, new services will also be concealed or part concealed behind suspended ceilings, wall claddings and column casings.

It is an inevitable aspect of fitting out works that original architectural features are concealed behind necessarily contemporary finishes. Within the proposed works, with the exception of the former Wylie & Lochhead part of the store, this will generally continue to be the case. Where practicable, original features outwith the Wylie & Lochhead area will be exposed. Within the Wylie & Lochhead area, original features will be exposed as a matter of principle.

It is not intended that any concealed features will be removed as a result of the works. Prior to commencing works in any area, the original building shell will be exposed and recording work undertaken as appropriate.

In terms of the relevant guidance, it is considered that by upgrading the historic use of the store the internal fit out works will enhance the special interest of the listed buildings in their historic use as a department store and provide substantial social, economic and cultural benefits to the wider community.

In terms of physical impact, the essential special architectural interest of the buildings will be unaffected by the works, in the case of the façades facing onto Buchanan Street and onto Mitchell Street, or enhanced, in the case of the interior of the former Wylie & Lochhead building. As with all of the works they will, in any event, be reversible.

Reconfiguration of entrance and installation of new shopfronts on corner of Argyle Street/Buchanan Street

It is proposed to return the Argyle Street/Buchanan Street corner to the general configuration which predated its alteration in the 1930s (Figures 3.17b and c). It is intended that this will remove the present visually and physically awkward corner entrance (Figure 3.14).

The present shop front configuration is not original and is not an element of special architectural or historic interest.

In this respect, in terms of the relevant guidance, it is considered that the reconfiguration will have little or no impact on the special interest of the listed building at 134–156 Argyle Street and 3–7 Buchanan Street.

Replacement of existing entrances with new glass doors and black tiled surrounds

None of the present entrances is original. All derive from previous alterations undertaken to create entrances of relevant contemporary appearance (Figures 3.7, 3.9 and 3.14).

The proposals will create relevant, consistent, high-quality entrances across the entire store frontage (Figures 3.17a–e).

In terms of the relevant guidance, the replacement of the outdated entrance doors with contemporary entrances will have no physical affect upon the special interest of the listed buildings and will be highly beneficial to continuing their historic use as a department store.

In each case they are reversible and in turn will be replaced under future cycles of refurbishment.

Replacement of existing shop windows with new single-pane windows in black aluminium frames

The existing shop windows are not original although, in the case of 21–31 Buchanan Street, there are original cast iron sub-divisional elements that will be unaffected. In this respect these works are specifically of a 'like for like' nature (Figures 3.17a–e).

Local design guidelines relating to the replacement of shop fronts in the city centre have informed the design process.

Again, in terms of the relevant guidance, the replacement of the outdated shop windows with contemporary windows will have no physical affect upon the special interest of the listed buildings and is in any event reversible, and they in turn will be replaced under future cycles of refurbishment.

Provision of new fascia/signage in black stove enamelled aluminium with illuminated lettering

The installation of a high-quality fascia across all of the frontages (with the exception of the former Wylie & Lochhead frontage) will improve the appearance of the existing dado, which is in many cases not original and consequently of variable quality. It is an essential part of signalling the store (Figures 3.17a–e).

A variety of different fascias have been applied to the buildings throughout their history (Figures 3.6–3.9 and 3.13–3.16). The proposed unifying fascia will have little or no impact upon the special interest of the listed buildings.

Install flags/banners in existing sockets

Sockets for flags exist at the façades of the buildings. They are not original but clearly must have been used at some point during the evolution of the present store.

The installation of flags/banners along the store frontage will be a relevant means of signalling the store and the foot of Buchanan Street in general. In this respect it will enliven the street and attract shoppers, to the general benefit of Buchanan Street.

The proposed flags/banners are by their very nature temporary in appearance and if anything will accentuate and enhance the special interest of the listed façades (Figures 3.17a–e).

Summary

The proposed works have been devised to signal the upgraded store as a House of Fraser flagship store of the very highest quality.

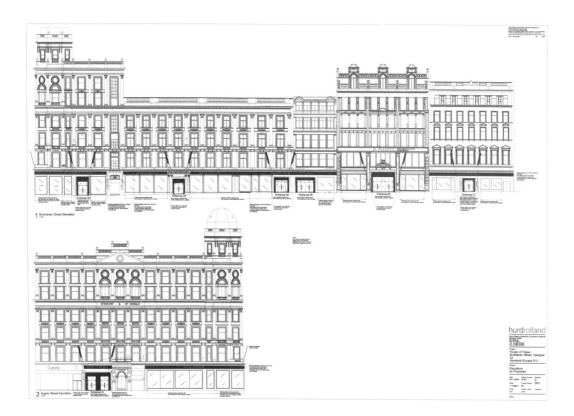

3.17a

**Elevations showing
proposed alterations
(courtesy of Hurd
Rolland/Havelock
Europa)**

3.17b

**134–156 Argyle
Street (proposed)
(courtesy of Hurd
Rolland Partnership/
Havelock Europa)**

3.17c
3–7 Buchanan Street (proposed)
(courtesy of Hurd Rolland Partnership/
Havelock Europa)

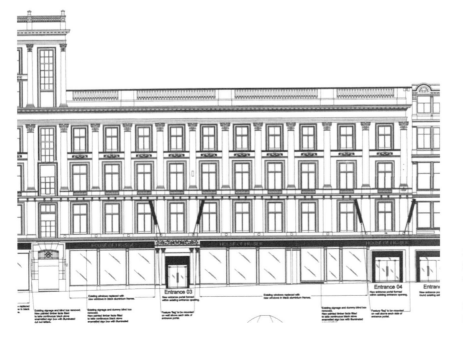

3.17d
21–31 Buchanan
Street (proposed)
(courtesy of Hurd
Rolland Partnership/
Havelock Europa)

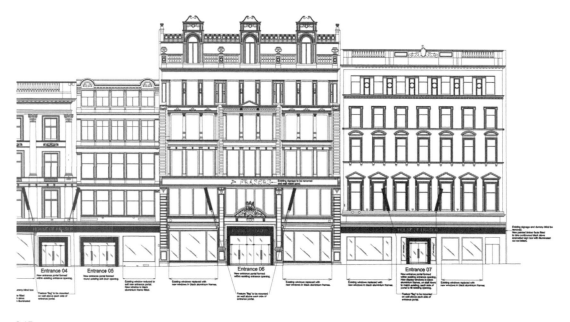

3.17e
45 Buchanan Street (proposed) (courtesy of Hurd Rolland Partnership/Havelock Europa)

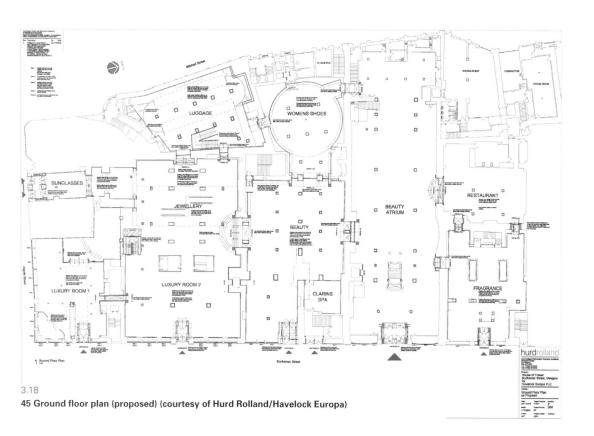

3.18
45 Ground floor plan (proposed) (courtesy of Hurd Rolland/Havelock Europa)

Internally, the proposals represent either a high-quality 'like for like' replacement of the existing fit out or the improvement of access through the store. Externally, they continue the principle of creating a unifying identity whilst acknowledging the diversity of the clearly individual façadal elements.

In terms of relevant guidance, the works will have little or no physical impact upon the special interest of any of the listed buildings. Rather, the proposals will accentuate the store's present function as an essential anchor at the foot of Buchanan Street and will potentially provide considerable social, economic and cultural benefits to the wider community.

Architectural elements and features of a lesser interest may be partially or completely concealed by the proposed works but where still intact will be retained in place. In this respect the proposed works are essentially reversible.

Executive summary

A concluding section within the Heritage Statement summarized all of the above:

Executive summary and conclusion

Introduction

House of Fraser are undertaking a major refit of their premises in Buchanan Street as part of a long-term commitment to maintaining a high-quality department store in the city where they were originally founded.

The present store has been formed by the amalgamation of a number of individual retail premises within the Central Conservation Area, incorporating 3 Listed Buildings:

134–156 Argyle Street and 3–7 Buchanan Street	Category B Listed	Figs 3.1b, c & 3.3b
21–31 Buchanan Street	Category A Listed	Figs 3.1d & 3.3c
45 Buchanan Street	Category A Listed	Figs 3.1e & 3.3d

Glasgow City Council have advised that Listed Building consent is required for the works.

National policy

The upgrading of shops, offices and other such uses, that are reliant upon high-quality contemporary appearance as an essential part of their business, is a key economic driver for maintaining and enhancing the historic environment.

Current national policy and guidance recognises that change that will maintain and enhance what is important within the historic environment can provide wider social and economic benefits to the local community.

In this respect, in relation to works affecting listed buildings, the key factors are:

- the assessment of what is of special architectural or historic interest;
- the specific scale of any impact on this special interest set against any social, economic and cultural benefits to the wider community;
- where appropriate, the reversibility of the works.

Special interest

With the exception of the former Wylie & Lochhead building, the special architectural interest of the listed buildings that comprise the present-day House of Fraser Store essentially relates to their individual façades, generally from first-floor level upwards facing out onto Buchanan Street and Argyle Street (and in some cases onto Mitchell Street).

In relation to the former Wylie & Lochhead building, the special architectural interest extends to its façades on both Buchanan Street and Mitchell Street and to the original interior architectural features of the building and, most importantly, the mahogany staircase, the five-storey gallery and the glass roof over. In this respect, some presently concealed architectural features are likely to be of some interest.

The sub-divisional elements and original architectural features within the other areas of the store have some importance as a record of the store's evolution from the various essentially utilitarian building forms that predated the merging of the buildings at 21–31 and 45 Buchanan Street.

Scale of impact

The proposed works have been devised to signal the upgraded store as a House of Fraser flagship store of the very highest quality.

Internally, the proposals represent either a high-quality 'like for like' replacement of the existing fit out or the improvement of access through the store. Externally, they continue the principle of creating a unifying identity whilst acknowledging the diversity of the clearly individual façadal elements.

In terms of relevant guidance, the works will have little or no physical impact upon the special interest of any of the listed buildings. Rather the proposals will accentuate the store's present function as an essential anchor at the foot of Buchanan Street and will potentially provide considerable social, economic and cultural benefits to the wider community.

Reversibility

Architectural elements and features of a lesser interest may be partially or completely concealed by the proposed works but where still intact will be retained in place. In this respect the proposed works are essentially reversible.

Conclusions

The works proposed by House of Fraser will have little or no physical impact on the special architectural and historic interest of the listed buildings and will provide significant social, economic and cultural benefits to the City Centre at this location. In this regard the proposals reflect national (and, by association, local) conservation policy, and Listed Building consent should be granted.

The Glasgow City Plan incorporates specific design policy in relation to shop fronts, signage and other relevant issues. These matters will be material considerations in relation to approving planning consent for the works.

Summary

Realistically, there was little doubt that the proposed upgrading of the existing store, in the form undertaken, would be given Planning and Listed Building consent. The cyclical refurbishment of such historic buildings is an essential part of their long-term future use. In this instance, the issue was more to do with demonstrating that the special interest of the Category A and B Listed Buildings had been properly considered, in terms of the Planning (Listed Buildings and Conservation Areas) (Scotland) Act 1997.

The provision of the Heritage Statement justifying the work in terms of the relevant guidance was sufficient to enable the local authority to demonstrate that it had met its statutory obligations.

Conclusion

There is a substantial amount of formal guidance provided in relation to properly addressing the requirements of the Planning (Listed Buildings and Conservation Areas) Acts. It is this guidance that is the basis for any case that is to be made in relation to development or regeneration that will affect Listed Buildings and Conservation Areas.

The guidance provides those involved in development and design for heritage sensitive sites with a clear opportunity to take the initiative in approaching local authority planners. There are rarely sufficient resources available to local authorities, or indeed the key heritage bodies, to enable bespoke heritage assessments to be undertaken in relation to specific applications. Consequently, it is to the advantage of both the developer and the relevant planning authorities for the developer to take the initiative in promoting a coherent and clearly assessed heritage case.

The heritage case should evolve alongside the design of any proposal. However, in its final form, it should be presented as a stand alone supporting statement of intent specifically justified on the basis of the existing formal guidance. Thereafter, it is for those responsible for making the planning decision either to accept or reject the case being made.

Ultimately, it is the duty of the planning decision-maker to have special regard toward the desirability of preserving the historic built environment. The provision of a properly prepared heritage case should demonstrate this special regard and make it very much less likely that any planning decision involving heritage matters be called in and subsequently overturned.

Index